THE LUKAN PASSION AND THE PRAISEWORTHY DEATH

New Testament Monographs, 10

Series Editor
Stanley E. Porter

THE LUKAN PASSION AND THE PRAISEWORTHY DEATH

Peter J. Scaer

SHEFFIELD PHOENIX PRESS

2005

Published by Sheffield Phoenix Press
Department of Biblical Studies, University of Sheffield
Sheffield S10 2TN

www.sheffieldphoenix.com

A CIP catalogue record for this book
is available from the British Library

Typeset by Forthcoming Publications
Printed on acid-free paper by Lightning Source

ISBN 1-905048-24-6
ISSN 1747-9606

CONTENTS

Acknowledgments

Much of what is good in this work, I owe to my friend and mentor, Jerome Neyrey. As my 'Barnabas', his generous spirit and encouragement carried me through many a dark day. I should also like to express a word of gratitude to Harry Attridge, Gregory Sterling, John Cavadini, and all the folks at Notre Dame who did their best to make me a scholar. Thanks also belong to my supportive colleagues at Concordia Theological Seminary, including, happily, my father, whose best teaching has always been by example. I should also add that along the way to publication, such folks as Larry and Grace Beane, Justin Kane, Robert Smith, and Duncan Burns, have often come to my rescue. Finally, I bow to my wife Amy, who puts up with me and supports me in so many ways. Without her, I would be truly hopeless.

ABBREVIATIONS

AB	Anchor Bible
ABRL	Anchor Bible Reference Library
AnBib	Analecta biblica
ANRW	Hildegard Temporini and Wolfgang Haase (eds.), *Aufstieg und Niedergang der römischen Welt: Geschichte und Kultur Roms im Spiegel der neueren Forschung* (Berlin: W. de Gruyter, 1972–)
Bib	*Biblica*
BK	*Bibel und Kirche*
CBQ	*Catholic Biblical Quarterly*
CBQMS	*Catholic Biblical Quarterly*, Monograph Series
ETL	*Ephemerides theologicae lovanienses*
HTR	*Harvard Theological Review*
JBL	*Journal of Biblical Literature*
JJS	*Journal of Jewish Studies*
JSNT	*Journal for the Study of the New Testament*
JSNTSup	*Journal for the Study of the New Testament*, Supplement Series
JTS	*Journal of Theological Studies*
LingBib	*Linguistica Biblica*
NovT	*Novum Testamentum*
NTS	*New Testament Studies*
RAC	*Reallexikon für Antike und Christentum*
SBLDS	SBL Dissertation Series
SBLMS	SBL Monograph Series
SBLSP	SBL Seminar Papers
SBLTT	SBL Texts and Translations
SNT	Studien zum Neuen Testament
SNTSMS	Society for New Testament Studies Monograph Series
TDNT	Gerhard Kittel and Gerhard Friedrich (eds.), *Theological Dictionary of the New Testament* (trans. Geoffrey W. Bromiley; 10 vols.; Grand Rapids: Eerdmans, 1964–)
ThViat	*Theologia Viatorum*
TJT	*Toronto Journal of Theology*
ZNW	*Zeitschrift für die neutestamentliche Wissenschaft*

1

Introduction

1. *The Shame of Crucifixion in the Ancient World*

In the ancient world crucifixion epitomized shame and humiliation.[1] Death on the cross symbolized all that which was criminal,[2] foreign,[3] servile,[4] and lowly. Those crucified included bandits, prisoners of war, revolutionaries, and murderers. Crucifixion was most especially the punishment of society's marginalized, including rebellious slaves and foreigners. For the ancients, it was axiomatic that 'every malefactor (ἕκαστος κακούργων) condemned to death bears his cross on his back' (Plutarch, *Delay* 554B). As the supreme punishment of the Roman Empire, crucifixion was the antithesis of all that the Greco-Roman world held to be noble, honorable, and praiseworthy.

Indeed, crucifixion stood not simply as a most painful punishment, but as a public spectacle of humiliation.[5] This humiliation might begin

1. Martin Hengel, *Crucifixion: In the Ancient World and Folly of the Message of the Cross* (Philadelphia: Fortress Press, 1977). See also J. Massyngbaerde Ford, *Redeemer: Friend and Mother: Salvation in Antiquity and in the Gospel of John* (Minneapolis: Fortress Press, 1997), esp. 52-58; Joseph Fitzmyer, 'Crucifixion in Ancient Palestine, Qumran Literature, and the New Testament', *CBQ* 40 (1978), 493-513; Raymond Brown, *The Death of the Messiah: From Gethsemane to the Grave* (2 vols.; Garden City, NY: Doubleday, 1994), I, 95-97.

2. Seneca calls the cross the 'criminal wood' (*Ep.* 101.14). Unless otherwise indicated, translations of classical authors are taken from the Loeb Classical Library (Cambridge, MA: Harvard University Press).

3. Cicero says that the very word 'cross' should be 'far removed not only from the person of a Roman citizen, but his thought, eyes, and ears' (*Rab. Perd.* 16).

4. Cicero calls crucifixion the *servitutis extremum summumque supplicium* (*Verr.* 2.5.169). Plautus writes of the 'terrible cross' of slaves (*Poen.* 347). Tacitus refers to crucifixion as a 'slave-type' (*servile modum*) punishment (*Hist.* 2.72.1-2). See also Quintilian, *Institutio Oratoria* 4.2.17.

5. For a handy summary of the various steps of humiliation involved in crucifixion, see Jerome Neyrey's 'Despising the Shame of the Cross: Honor and Shame in the Johannine Passion Narrative', *Semeia* 68 (1996), 113-37 (113-14).

with a show trial, during which the condemned would be disgraced in a public forum.[6] Crucifixion was often preceded by public flogging and other forms of torture, which served to disfigure the body.[7] Then the accused would carry his own cross to the site of the execution (Plutarch, *Delay* 554B). Accordingly, crosses were often placed in public places and on busy roads to ensure a good crowd. Indeed, crucifixion became a form of public entertainment (see Philo's *Flacc.* 84-85). Victims were stripped naked, so as to expose their shame (see Diodorus Siculus 33.15.1). There, the condemned would be left to die an often slow death. Seneca writes:

> Can anyone be found who would prefer wasting away in pain dying limb by limb, or letting out his life drop by drop, rather than expiring once for all? Can any man be found willing to be fastened to an accursed tree (*infelix lignum*), long sickly, already deformed, swelling with ugly welts on shoulders and chest, and drawing the breath of life amid long-drawn-out agony. He would have many excuses for dying before mounting the cross. (*Dialogi* 3)

As we learn from Seneca, crucifixion's shame is made greater by the disfiguring of the naked body, which loses its beauty and natural dignity and forfeits its autonomy in the long, painful process of dying. After death, the bodies would often be left hanging as carrion for the vultures. This public exposure and lack of burial punctuated the public humiliation of the crucifixion (see Juvenal, *Satires* 14.77-78). As Epictetus says, 'It is not a terrible thing to die, but to die shamefully (αἰσχρῶς)'[8] (*Diatr.* 2.1.13). There was no shame worse than that of dying on the cross.

2. *The Shame of the Cross and Early Christian Apologetics*

Given its public and humiliating nature, crucifixion carried with it a social stigma, which labeled those crucified as shameful and blameworthy. In the context of this most negative stereotype, Jesus' death by crucifixion was an offense to the prevailing social values of the Greco-Roman world. This fact is attested to by such early Christian writers as Paul, who calls the crucified Christ a 'stumbling-block' (σκάνδαλον) to the Jews and 'foolishness' (μωρίαν) for the Gentiles (1 Cor. 1.23). He further refers to Jesus' death on a cross as the

6. On this point, see Cicero, *Rab. Perd.* 9–17.

7. For examples of such torture, see Josephus (*War* 5.549-551) who tells us that Jewish fugitives were 'first whipped, and then tormented with all sorts of tortures'. See also Livy, *History* 22.13.19; Seneca, *De ira* 3.6.

8. Author's translation.

ultimate self-humiliation (Phil. 2.8). Likewise, the author of Hebrews writes explicitly of the cross's shame (αἰσχύνης) (Heb. 12.2).

Not surprisingly, the ignominy of the cross became a focal point for opponents of Christianity. Justin Martyr, for instance, had to defend Christianity for the 'madness' (μανία) of honoring a crucified man as second only to God himself (*1 Apol.* 13.4). Origen took great pains to answer Celsus' charges that Jesus was 'bound in a most ignominious fashion' and 'executed in a most shameful way (αἴχιστα)' (*Cels.* 6.10). Similarly, Lactantius had to explain why God did not allow Jesus to die an honorable type of death (*honestum...mortis genus*) (*Inst.* 4.26.29).

3. *Luke as an Apologist for the Crucifixion*

The shame of crucifixion was clearly on Luke's mind, especially as he was defending Christianity's place within the larger Greco-Roman world. Within the New Testament, Luke–Acts stands at the forefront of Christian apologetics.[9] Luke was intent on demonstrating that Christianity did not arise 'in a corner', but was a proud, indeed ancient religion, whose founder was an honorable benefactor and savior (cf. Acts 10.38).[10] As part of his apologetic thrust Luke intended to demonstrate that Jesus' death was, in fact, honorable and praiseworthy. In order to establish this, Luke would have to overcome certain obstacles and stereotypes. He had to present Jesus as noble and praiseworthy in spite of the fact that he was arrested as a revolutionary, mocked, beaten, and crucified. A formidable task!

4. *The Noble Death:* Status Quaestionis

Just as the ancients held crucifixion to be most shameful, conversely they recognized that some deaths were especially noble, honorable, and praiseworthy.[11] A death met courageously brought glory. The

9. See, for instance, H.J. Cadbury, *The Making of Luke–Acts* (Peabody, MA: Hendrickson, 1958), 306-16; also Robert O'Toole, 'Luke's Position on Politics and Society in Luke–Acts', in Richard Cassidy and Phillip Scharper (eds.), *Political Issues in Luke–Acts* (Maryknoll, NY: Orbis Books, 1983), 1-17.

10. See Abraham Malherbe, '"Not in a Corner": Early Christian Apologetic in Acts 26.26', *The Second Century* 5 (1985–86), 193-210. For discussion of Jesus as Greco-Roman benefactor, see Frederick Danker's *Jesus and the New Age* (Philadelphia: Fortress Press, 1988), esp. 2-10.

11. The study of noble/honorable death is intimately related to the study of honor and shame in the ancient world. For seminal studies in this regard, see

warrior Achilles captures the spirit of the heroic death: 'If I stay here and fight beside the city of the Trojans, my return home is gone, but my glory is everlasting' (Homer, *Il.* 9.412-13). Likewise, Isocrates described the noble death as 'the special honor which nature has preserved for the noble' (*Oratore* 1.43).

Seminal studies addressing the ancients' understanding of noble death include those of A. Ronconi and H.A. Musurillo.[12] Ronconi's 'Exitus illustrium virorum' traces the literary history of great men who stood up for what they believed in the face of tyranny by the state. Musurillo, especially in his appendix on the tradition of martyr literature, offers a brief but helpful overview of the historical relationships between Socrates, the so-called Maccabean, pagan, and Christian martyrs.[13]

A number of monographs have appeared more recently which further our understanding of the noble death in the ancient world. David Seeley, drawing upon the Maccabean literature and such Greco-Roman authors as Seneca, Epictetus, and Plutarch, argues that Paul made use of the Greco-Roman tradition of noble death in order to depict Jesus' death as vicarious.[14] One need not agree with his conclusion to appreciate the fact that Seeley lays bare a noble death tradition which can be found in the Maccabean literature, and which has its roots in the Greco-Roman thought-world. Though their work is at its heart an apology for suicide, A.J. Droge and J.D. Tabor likewise have assembled an impressive array of material which demonstrates that the noble death tradition was widespread and enduring in the ancient world.[15] David A. deSilva in his study on the epistle to the Hebrews has taken the question a step further by demonstrating that the questions of honor and shame, foundational to an under-

Bruce Malina, *The New Testament World: Insights from Cultural Anthropology* (Louisville, KY: Westminster/John Knox Press, rev. edn, 1993), 28-62. See also Bruce Malina and Jerome Neyrey, 'Honor and Shame in Luke–Acts', in Jerome Neyrey (ed.), *The Social World of Luke–Acts: Models for Interpretation* (Peabody, MA: Hendrickson, 1991), 25-66.

12. See Alessandro Ronconi, 'Exitus illustrium virorum', *RAC* 6 (1966), 1258-66; H.A. Musurillo, *The Acts of the Pagan Martyrs: Acta Alexandrinorum* (Oxford: Oxford University Press, 1954; repr. edn, New York: Arno, 1979).

13. Musurillo, *Acts of the Pagan Martyrs*, 236-46.

14. David Seeley, *The Noble Death: Graeco-Roman Martyrology and Paul's Concept of Salvation* (JSNTSup, 28; Sheffield: JSOT Press, 1989).

15. Arthur J. Droge and James D. Tabor, *A Noble Death: Suicide and Martyrdom among Christians and Jews in Antiquity* (San Francisco: HarperSanFrancisco, 1992).

standing of a noble death, are deeply embedded within the rhetoric of Greco-Roman culture.[16]

A parallel study to part of this work can be found in Jerome Neyrey's *Honor and Shame in the Gospel of Matthew*, in which the author argues that Matthew drew upon the rhetoric of praise to depict Jesus' life and death as both noble and praiseworthy.[17] Also important in this regard is Adela Collins's article 'From Noble Death to Crucified Messiah', which addresses the difficulty that Mark faced in presenting a crucified Savior to a culture familiar with the noble death tradition.[18] This study likewise will focus on an evangelist's use of the noble death tradition.

5. *Noble Death and the Lukan Passion:* Status Quaestionis

Scholars have long recognized that the Lukan passion narrative differs in significant ways from that of Matthew and Mark. Luke portrays Jesus as a man who is especially courageous, pious, and willing to die. Even in death, the Lukan Jesus remains in control of his surroundings, and continues to offer his blessings.[19] Redaction critics in particular have persuasively argued that these emphases are primarily a product of Luke's own editorial reshaping.[20] The next question is: What resources did Luke draw upon to shape his passion narrative in the way that he did?

A number of scholars have traced the uniqueness of the Lukan passion to the martryological tradition. Martin Dibelius was among the first who argued that the Lukan passion offers Christians a 'model of innocent suffering'.[21] Charles Talbert, among others, holds that through his use of martryological themes Luke aimed to present Christ as a person to be admired for his 'selfless commitment'.[22]

16. David A. deSilva, *Despising Shame: Honor Discourse and Community Maintenance in the Epistle to the Hebrews* (SBLDS, 152; Atlanta: Scholars Press, 1995).

17. Jerome Neyrey, *Honor and Shame in the Gospel of Matthew* (Louisville, KY: Westminster/John Knox Press, 1998), 70-163.

18. Adele Y. Collins, 'From Noble Death to Crucified Messiah', *NTS* 40 (1994), 481-503.

19. For a brief survey of special Lukan features in the passion narrative, see Brown, *Death of the Messiah*, I, 67-75.

20. For a helpful summary of scholars on both sides of the issue, see Brown, *Death of the Messiah*, I, 66-67.

21. Martin Dibelius, *From Tradition to Gospel* (London: Macmillan, 1934), 201.

22. Charles Talbert, 'Martyrdom in Luke–Acts and the Lukan Social Ethic', in Cassidy and Scharper (eds.), *Political Issues in Luke–Acts*, 99-110 (106).

More recently, John Kloppenborg and Gregory Sterling have tendered articles in which they argue that the noble death tradition, especially as embodied in the story of Socrates, played a significant role in the shaping of Luke's passion narrative.[23] They contend that Socrates was not simply a major source of the noble death tradition, but that Luke made use specifically of the Socrates figure to portray Jesus' death as noble. Their exploratory articles, I think, merit our consideration.

One source has yet to be fully considered: namely, the Greco-Roman values of a praiseworthy death as embedded in rhetoric. As we shall see, the study of formal rhetoric was fundamentally linked to the acquisition of literacy. Moreover, rhetoric carried within it many of the tools which Luke would need for removing the cross's shame and replacing it with the honor of noble death. Exploring the place of the rhetorical values in the Lukan passion takes seriously the fact that Luke—notwithstanding his immersion in Jewish history and his knowledge of the Old Testament—wrote in Greek to a Hellenized audience. Up to this point, some have touched upon the issue, but no one has addressed it in a systematic fashion. A thorough study of Luke's use of the resources and motifs of noble death, as found in rhetoric, needs to be made.

6. *Luke's Education and Social Status*

Before embarking upon such a study, we need to take inventory of Luke as a Greco-Roman writer of some skill, knowledge, and social status within the Greco-Roman world. By considering his level of education, we may have a better grasp as to the resources he was able to draw upon in fashioning his passion account.

The scholarly consensus has changed dramatically from the days in which the Gospel writers were considered little more than primitive recorders of oral tradition. Increasingly, scholars have recognized that the so-called *Kleinliteratur* (popular literature) of the New Testament is not so far removed from the *Hochliteratur* (cultivated literature) of the ancient world's upper classes.[24] The evangelists are

23. John Kloppenborg, '"Exitus clari viri": The Death of Jesus in Luke', *TJT* 8 (1992), 106-20; Gregory Sterling, 'Mors Philosophi: The Death of Jesus in Luke', *HTR* 94 (2001), 383-402.

24. For a discussion of the changes in scholarly attitudes towards the New Testament writings, see David Aune, *The New Testament in its Literary Environment* (Philadelphia: Westminster Press, 1987), esp. 11-14.

theologians and sophisticated editors of the Gospel material. Luke tells us that Peter and John were dismissed as 'unlettered' (ἀγράμματοι) (Acts 4.13), but the third evangelist clearly does not fit this description.[25] He shows himself to be a cosmopolitan writer of above-average social status and educational background.

To place Luke within the social world of his time, we would do well briefly to catalogue what he knows, as evidenced by his writings. Vernon Robbins, in his 'The Social Location of the Implied Author of Luke–Acts', offers a fresh, complex picture of Luke's social status.[26] Robbins demonstrates that Luke's numerous skills and abilities are evidence of his high social status. For starters, the third evangelist shows himself a master of the historian's tools, as he is able to draw upon written and oral reports to create a document for public consumption (Lk. 1.1-4). Luke also demonstrates his easy familiarity of the political situation, placing his story within the larger framework of such leaders as Caesar Augustus (Lk. 2.1), Tiberius Caesar (Lk. 3.1), and Claudius (Acts 18.2). Furthermore, he displays a knowledge of geography which encompasses the entire Empire, from Ethiopia (Acts 8.26-39) to Cyrenaica (Acts 2.10). Luke mentions some thirty cities specifically.[27] Luke also demonstrates that he is acquainted with the social stratification of his day. Luke's world is inhabited by people of every social status, including emperors (Lk. 2.1), kings and queens (Lk. 11.31; Acts 12.1), prefects and proconsuls (Acts 13.7), city-dwellers (Lk. 7.37-50), widows (Acts 9.39), and slave girls (Acts 16.16-18). Finding its way into Luke's work is a remarkable ethnic mix, which includes Galileans, Parthians, Medes, Elamites, Cretans, Arabs, and Romans, among others (see Acts 2.5-11). The

25. Luke uses the astonishment of people at Peter and John's lack of education as a literary device. See Hans Conzelmann, *Acts of the Apostles: A Commentary on the Acts of the Apostles* (trans. James Limburg, A. Thomas Kraabel, and Donald H. Juel; Philadelphia: Fortress Press, 1987), 33.

26. Vernon K. Robbins, 'The Social Location of the Implied Author of Luke–Acts', in Neyrey (ed.), *The Social World of Luke–Acts*, 305-32. For an earlier discussion of Luke's knowledge of the world, a good resource can be found in Colin J. Hemer's *The Book of Acts in the Setting of Hellenistic History* (Tübingen: J.C.B. Mohr, 1989), esp. 101-58.

27. See Richard Rohrbaugh, 'The Pre-industrial City in Luke–Acts', in Neyrey (ed.), *The Social World of Luke–Acts*, 125-49 (126). James M. Scott ('Luke's Geographical Horizon', in David W.J. Gill and Conrad Gempf [eds.], *The Book of Acts in its Graeco-Roman Setting* [*The Book of Acts in its First Century Setting*, 2; Grand Rapids: Eerdmans, 1994], 483-544) argues persuasively that Luke's geographical horizon is a confluence of both the Jewish and the Greco-Roman world-views.

author further displays knowledge of various technologies, from the production of tents (Acts 18.1-3) and the work of silversmiths (Acts 19.23), to the various techniques of sailing a ship through rough weather (Acts 27.1-20). Likewise, the author portrays himself as one who is an 'insider', not only within the Christian movement, but within society as a whole. As an insider within the Christian movement, he knows the accounts of Jesus' life that have been written before his own (Lk. 1.1). The literary prefaces, addressed to the 'most excellent Theophilus', place the writer in the honored position of retainer to a wealthy man. Robbins further demonstrates that Luke is 'bi-cultural', a man who is at home in Jewish culture and history, but is able, likewise, to write a stylized Greco-Roman preface and quote the occasional Greek poet (Acts 17.28). Robbins proceeds to demonstrate that Luke has a working knowledge of various belief systems and ideologies, including the political–military–legal system of the day. He knows, moreover, the basic philosophical positions of the Stoics and Epicureans (Acts 17). Likewise, he recognizes the important roles played by such officials as tribunes (Lysias, Acts 21–23), proconsuls (see Sergius Paulus, Acts 13.6-12), and Asiarchs (Acts 19.31). Thus, from Luke's own writings, we see that he presents himself as a cosmopolitan author of some cultural sophistication.[28]

We may also consider the number of literary forms which Luke appears to have in his authorial arsenal. David Aune notes the following literary forms found in Luke–Acts: historical prefaces (Lk. 1.1-4; Acts 1.1-5), genealogy (Lk. 3.23-38), symposia (Lk. 5.27-32; 7.36-50; 11.37-54; 14.1-24), travel narratives (Lk. 9.51–19.44; Acts 12.25–21.16; 27.1–28.16), speeches (32 in the book of Acts, 13 of which are significant in length), letters (Acts 15.23-29; 23.26-30), dramatic episodes (Lk. 4.16-30 and 24.13-35, for instance), and summaries (Lk. 1.80; 2.40, 52; 4.14, 37, 40-41; 6.17-19; 7.17, 21; 9.6; Acts 2.43-47; 4.32-35; 5.11-16, for instance).[29] We will have to come back to a number of these literary forms in due course, but evidence suggests once again that Luke is a writer of some sophistication.

Luke's sophistication can be further seen in his extensive use of literary patterning, which includes the parallel stories of John the

28. For further discussion of Luke's knowledge of ancient geography, politics, and the military, see Marion Soards, 'The Historical and Cultural Setting of Luke and Acts', in Earl Richard (ed.), *New Views on Luke and Acts* (Collegeville, MN: Liturgical Press [A Michael Glazier Book], 1990), 33-47. See also Scott's 'Luke's Geographical Horizon'.

29. Aune, *The New Testament and its Literary Environment*, 120-31.

Baptist and Jesus in Luke,[30] as well the literary patterns which link Luke to Acts. Distinct cases of such literary linkage include (1) the deaths of Jesus and Stephen, (2) Jesus' resurrection appearance and Peter's miraculous release from prison, (3) the farewell speeches of Jesus and Paul, (4) the journey of Jesus to Jerusalem and Paul's journey to Jerusalem and Rome, (5) the trials of Jesus and Paul.[31]

Luke's literary patterning may also be seen within the book of Acts itself, where Luke draws parallels between the ministries of Peter and Paul: (1) both heal cripples (3.2-8; 14.8-12), (2) both heal by their personal presence, Peter by shadow, Paul by clothes (5.15; 19.12), (3) both have encounters with sorcerers (8.18; 13.6), (4) both perform resurrection-type miracles (9.36; 20.9), (5) both are miraculously released from prison (12.7; 16.26). Luke here employs what the ancient rhetorical handbooks refer to as 'comparisons', by which one figure is praised in light of another esteemed person.[32] These couplets again demonstrate that Luke is an author capable of creating a literary work of thematic and structural complexity.

Given the evidence of Luke's own writing, and his knowledge of the political world and its social structures, we are left to conclude that the third evangelist was a cultured and cosmopolitan writer of some sophistication, capable of drawing inspiration from many and varied resources.

7. *Resources at Luke's Disposal: Turning Shame into Honor*

Given the shameful stigma of the crucifixion, Luke's own apologetic interests, and his level of education within the Greco-Roman world, we may ask upon what resources Luke drew to mark Jesus' death as noble and praiseworthy.

This study will examine three possible sources. First, I will catalog the cultural values of a praiseworthy death, especially as embedded in Greco-Roman rhetoric. This investigation of rhetoric should prove especially helpful, for it is here that we discern the bedrock values of the ancient world, as the ancients themselves articulate such values. Rhetoric will provide us with what social scientists refer to as an

30. For a handy summary of the way in which Luke compares John and Jesus, see Joseph Fitzmyer, *The Gospel according to Luke* (AB, 28, 28A; 2 vols.; Garden City, NY: Doubleday, 1981), I, 313-14.

31. For a study of Luke's use of literary patterns, see Robert C. Tannehill's *The Narrative Unity of Luke–Acts: A Literary Interpretation* (Philadelphia: Fortress Press, 1986).

32. For example, see Aristotle, *Rhetoric* 1.9.40.

emic, that is, native understanding of honor and praise in the ancient world. As part of my study of rhetoric, I will look at formal rhetoric. Then I will investigate how this rhetoric was put to use in funeral orations and in Plutarch's *Lives*. Secondly, I will investigate the possibility that Luke knew the story of Socrates, and alluded to his death in order to depict Jesus as a wise and courageous philosopher. As we will see, the figure of Socrates loomed large in the ancient mind, and served as a prime exemplar of noble death for centuries to come. Thirdly, I will question whether the Jewish martyrological tradition, as evidenced by the Maccabean literature and Josephus, played a role in Luke's shaping of the passion narrative. The martyrological literature merits our attention, in so much as it mediated Greco-Roman notions of the praiseworthy death to the Jewish world. Finally, in the last chapter, I will draw these resources together and ask how they contribute to Luke's portrayal of the passion.

2

Greco-Roman Rhetoric of Death and the Lukan Passion

1. *Introduction*

In this chapter I will examine Greco-Roman rhetoric as a possible resource that Luke may have drawn upon in order to portray Jesus' death as noble and praiseworthy.

Among the ancients, rhetoric, the art of 'speaking well', permeated the culture. Formal rhetoric crystallized in Aristotle's influential *Rhetoric*, and continued to be refined and spread throughout the Roman world by the likes of Cicero and Quintilian.[1]

Higher education, while including science, music, and arts, consisted primarily of the study of rhetoric, the apex of classical education.[2] Even fledgling students learned to read and write according to rhetorical models. By the time of Luke the study of rhetoric was facilitated by rhetorical handbooks, known as progymnasmata.[3] The progymnasmata offered preliminary lessons in the study of basic grammar, as well as such simple rhetorical forms as sayings (χρεία), maxims (γνώμη), and narratives (διήγησις). At a young age, students learned encomiastic composition. As George Kennedy writes, 'The grammar-school exercises included the composition of encomia in praise of a person, place, or thing'.[4] The advanced student would

1. See George Kennedy, *The Art of Persuasion in Greece* (Princeton, NJ: Princeton University Press, 1963); *idem*, *The Art of Persuasion in the Roman World: 300 B.C.–A.D. 300* (Princeton, NJ: Princeton University Press, 1963); *idem*, *The Art of Rhetoric in the Roman World: 300 B.C.–A.D. 300* (Princeton, NJ: Princeton University Press, 1972). See also, Aubrey Gwynn, *Roman Education from Cicero to Quintilian* (Oxford: Clarendon Press, 1926).

2. See Stanley F. Bonner, *Education in Ancient Rome* (Berkeley, CA: University of California Press, 1977).

3. See Bonner, *Education in Ancient Rome*, 250-76; H.I. Marrou, *A History of Education in Antiquity* (New York: Sheed & Ward, 1956), 276-81.

4. George Kennedy, *New Testament Interpretation through Rhetorical Criticism* (Chapel Hill, NC: University of North Carolina Press, 1984), 75.

then learn the fine art of persuasion, to argue a case pro and contra, to employ pathos, logos, and ethos, and finally to construct speeches within the three basic types of rhetoric: judicial, deliberative, and epideictic.

In particular, I will look at four distinct types of Greco-Roman writings: (1) the formal rhetoric of Aristotle, and its legacy, (2) the extant Athenian funeral speeches, (3) the educational rhetoric of the progymnasmata, and (4) the rhetoric of death as it is evidenced in Plutarch's *Lives*. The formal rhetoric of Aristotle will provide a comprehensive picture of rhetoric and its functions as the ancients articulated them. The funeral speeches will prove helpful in that they employ especially the rhetoric of praise. Then, the study of the progymnasmata will help us understand how the formal rhetoric of the rhetoricians would have been passed down to students as they learned to write encomia and comparisons. Finally, Plutarch's *Lives* will offer evidence that rhetorical values and devices permeated other literary genres.

2. *Formal Rhetoric and the Rhetoric of Noble Death*

a. *Epideictic Rhetoric, Vehicle for Praise*

The ancients, from Aristotle to Quintilian, recognized and practiced three basic species of rhetoric: deliberative, forensic, and epideictic. Deliberative rhetoric, either hortatory or dissuasive, is largely a political exercise; it concerns itself with future action, and asks whether an action is expedient (Aristotle, *Rhet.* 1.3.3). Judicial rhetoric, which has its home in the legal system, concerns itself with the past, and asks whether an act was performed justly or unjustly (*Rhet.* 1.3.3). The third species, epideictic rhetoric, has its natural setting in ceremonial occasions, such as public festivals or funerals (*Rhet.* 1.3.3).[5] The question before the epideictic rhetor is whether a person is 'honourable or disgraceful' (*Rhet.* 1.3.5). As such, epideictic rhetoric concerns itself with the person's character (ἦθος), especially as that character is displayed in his actions. This third species of rhetoric especially concerns us, for it is the rhetoric which the ancients employed for describing what it is that makes an act noble, honorable, and praiseworthy. Epideictic is the rhetoric which the ancients employed for praising a noble death. As Aristotle writes:

5. George Kennedy, *A New History of Classical Rhetoric* (Princeton, NJ: Princeton University Press, 1994), 4. For a thorough treatment of epideictic literature, see Theodore Burgess, 'Epideictic Rhetoric', *Studies in Classical Philology* 3 (1902), 89-261; reprinted as *Epideictic Literature* (New York: Garland, 1987).

> Similarly, those who praise (ἐπαινοῦντες) or blame (ψέγοντες) do not consider whether what a man has done is expedient or harmful, but frequently make it a matter for praise (ἐπαίνῳ) that, disregarding his own interest, he performed some deed of honour (τι καλόν). For example, they praise (ἐπαινοῦσιν) Achilles because he went to the aid of his comrade Patroclus, knowing that he was fated to die (δεῖ αὐτὸν ἀποθανεῖν), although he might have lived (ἐξὸν ζῆν). To him such a death was more honourable (θάνατος κάλλιον), although life was more expedient. (*Rhet.* 1.3.6)

Here we appreciate that ancients employed epideictic rhetoric as the vehicle for praising a noble death. Courageous acts, performed for the sake of others, were considered especially praiseworthy. As we shall see, epideictic rhetoric offers a number of rules and standards by which to praise such a death.

b. *Praise and the Centrality of Virtue*

What, according to Aristotle, makes a person praiseworthy? Aristotle begins his discussion of epideictic rhetoric by linking praise to acts of virtue and nobility, while assigning blame to acts of vice and disgrace:

> We will next speak of virtue (ἀρετῆς) and vice (κακίας), and of noble (καλοῦ) and disgraceful (αἰσχροῦ), since they constitute the aim of one who praises (ἐπαινοῦντι) and one who blames (ψέγοντι). (*Rhet.* 1.9.1)

For the rhetorician especially the virtuous quality of an action makes it praiseworthy. Aristotle writes:

> The noble (καλόν), then, is that which being desirable (αἱρετόν) in itself, is at the same time worthy of praise (ἐπαινετόν), or which, being good (ἀγαθόν), is pleasant because it is good (ἀγαθόν). (*Rhet.* 1.9.3)

Virtuous acts, being by nature good, are therefore praiseworthy:

> If this is the noble (τὸ καλόν), then virtue (τὴν ἀρετήν) must of necessity be noble (καλόν), for, being good (ἀγαθόν), it is worthy of praise (ἐπαινετόν). (*Rhet.* 1.9.3-4)

That which is noble and good is necessarily in accordance with virtue. Aristotle summarizes the matter thus: 'Now praise is language that sets forth greatness of virtue (ἀρετῆς)' (*Rhet.* 1.9.33).

c. *The Public/Praiseworthy Dimension of Virtue*

That which is virtuous merits praise. Still, the term 'virtue' needs to be clarified. Among the ancients, ἀρετή could refer to a goodness or excellence of any kind, including (1) mastery in a certain field, or endowment with higher power, (2) glorious deeds, (3) manliness or martial valor, (4) merit, (5) fame, or (6) virtue, as a recognized excellence in moral goodness.[6] As such, the ancients did not wholly equate virtue with an inner moral goodness, but understood it to have a public dimension, linked closely to honor. This link between virtue and honor dates back to Homeric times. As Joseph Pearson writes, 'In Homer, arete does not denote a quality of character inherent in a man. There is never any discussion of hidden, unrealized arete, because it does not exist until it is recognized by others.'[7] With the passage of time, the term 'virtue' came to encompass such excellencies as magnanimity, liberality, prudence, and other such qualities necessary for social and political intercourse within the democratic city-state.[8] As such, virtue was not simply an inner moral goodness, but a recognizable eminence. For the ancients, virtue was a public excellence worthy of public praise.

d. *The Parts of Virtue*

Aristotle divides virtue into certain definable parts: 'Justice, courage, self-control, magnificence, magnanimity, liberality, gentleness, practical and speculative wisdom' (*Rhet.* 1.9.6). Aristotle briefly defines these virtues as follows (1.9.5-13):

> Righteousness (δικαιοσύνη): assigns each man his due in conformity with the law.
>
> Courage (ἀνδρεία): makes men perform noble acts in the midst of dangers according to the dictates of the law and in submission to it; the contrary is cowardice.
>
> Self-Control (σωφροσύνη): disposes men in regard to the pleasures of the body as the law prescribes; the contrary is licentiousness.
>
> Liberality (φιλανθρπωία): does good in many matters; the contrary is avarice.
>
> Magnanimity (μεγαλοψυχία): productive of great benefits; the contrary is little-mindedness.
>
> Magnificence (μεγαλοπρέπεια): produces greatness in matters of expenditure; the contraries are little-mindedness and meanness.
>
> Practical Wisdom (φρόνησις): a virtue of reason, which enables men to come to a wise decision in regard to good and evil things.

6. See Otto Bauernsseind, 'ἀρετή', in *TDNT*, I, 458-61.
7. See Lionel Pearson, *Popular Ethics in Ancient Greece* (Stanford, CA: Stanford University Press, 1962), 50.
8. Arthur Adkins, *Merit and Responsibility: A Study in Greek Values* (Chicago: University of Chicago Press, 1960), 156-63, 176-79.

Aristotle's definition of virtue and its component parts digests commonplace Greek teachings on the subject. He could afford to be succinct precisely because he is treading familiar ground. For the purpose of this study, two virtues merit our special attention: righteousness and courage.

Righteousness stands as the first of the cardinal virtues. Elsewhere, Pseudo-Aristotle defines righteousness (δικαιοσύνη) more fully:

> First among the claims of righteousness (δικαιοσύνης) are our duties to the gods, then our duties to the spirits, then those to country and parents, then to those departed; among these claims is piety (εὐσέβεια), which is either a part of righteousness or concomitant of it. Righteousness is also accompanied by holiness and truth and loyalty and hatred of wickedness. (*Virt. vit.* 5.2-3.20-24)

Within Pseudo-Aristotle's definition of righteousness, we see that the chief virtue of righteousness is shaped by a hierarchy of obligations to the gods, the spirits, country, parents, and the departed. Pseudo-Aristotle's definition is echoed by an important third-century CE author of progymnasmata, Menander Rhetor:

> The parts of justice (δικαιοσύνης) are piety (εὐσέβεια), fair dealing and reverence: piety toward the gods, fair dealing towards men, reverence toward the departed. Piety consists of two elements: being god-loved and god-loving. The former means being loved by the gods and receiving many blessings from them, the latter consists of loving the gods and having a relationship of friendship with them. (*Treatise* 1.361.17-25)[9]

Again, we see that righteousness includes the fulfillment of duties to the gods, to one's fellow man, and to the departed. Righteousness, as such, is an all-encompassing virtue by which a man might be known and judged. A righteous man stands in good stead before god and man, and is therefore worthy of great praise and honor.

The virtue of courage, we shall see, also plays a prominent role in the noble death tradition. We note that elsewhere, Pseudo-Aristotle also gives a fuller definition of courage, delineating its various aspects:

> To courage it belongs to be undismayed by fears of death and confident in alarms and brave in the face of dangers, and to prefer a fine death to base security, and to be a cause of victory. It also belongs to courage to labour and endure and play a manly part. Courage is accompanied by confidence and bravery and daring, and also by perseverance and endurance. (*Virt. vit.* 4.4)

9. *Menander Rhetor* (eds. D.A. Russell and Nigel Wilson; Oxford: Clarendon Press, 1981).

Courage entails bravery in the face of danger, as well as endurance and perseverance in the face of hardship. Definitions of the various virtues, especially righteousness and courage, will prove helpful as we take a closer look at the way authors use them in depicting a praiseworthy death.

e. *Virtuous People are Praised for Performing Virtuous Deeds*
At the core of Aristotle's definitions is the tenet that as a tree bears fruit, so praiseworthy virtue manifests itself in virtuous deeds (*Rhet.* 1.9.13). The character (ἦθος) of a man manifests itself in honorable actions: for 'praise is founded on actions' (1.9.32). Aristotle continues, 'Now praise is the language that sets forth greatness of virtue; hence it is necessary to show that a man's actions are virtuous' (1.9.33). Therefore, the rhetor will demonstrate a person's nobility by speaking of his noble actions, and he will praise a person's courage by recounting his courageous actions:

> For it is evident that whatever produces virtue, as it tends to it, must be noble, and so also must be what comes from virtue; for such are its signs and works. (*Rhet.* 1.9.13)

Acts of virtue, Aristotle informs us, give evidence that a person is himself virtuous.

f. *Criteria for Assessing Praiseworthy Deeds*
(1) *Praiseworthy deeds benefit others.* Aristotle further defines virtue according to its usefulness to others:

> Virtue, it would seem, is a faculty of providing and preserving good things, a faculty productive of many and great benefits (δύναμις εὐεργετικὴ πολλῶν καὶ μεγάλων), in fact, of all things in all cases. (*Rhet.* 1.9.4-5)

Especially praiseworthy are those deeds which are 'the cause of enjoyment to others' (1.9.23). Accordingly, a person acts nobly when he does it 'for the sake of his country, while neglecting his own interests' (1.9.17). A deed is particularly praiseworthy if it is 'naturally good', performed apart from 'selfish motives' (1.9.17). The virtuous person seeks 'honour rather than money' (1.9.16).

(2) *Victory merits praise.* Aristotle deemed 'victory' (νίκη) praiseworthy (*Rhet.* 1.9.25). Conversely, he held that defeat was the mark of shame. Accordingly, 'a courageous man ought not to allow himself to be beaten' (1.9.24).

(3) *Amplification.* Part and parcel of the rhetoric of praise is the technique of amplification (αὔξησις). The purpose of amplification is to increase the rhetorical effect and importance of a statement by intensifying the circumstances of an object or action. The technique of amplification is especially suited to epideictic rhetoric, 'whose subject is actions which are not disputed, so that all that remains to be done is to attribute beauty and importance to them' (*Rhet.* 1.9.40).

One way to amplify the worth of a person's action is to highlight the uniqueness of what he has done. Particularly memorable and praiseworthy are those achievements marked by their singularity, for instance, if someone is the only one to have accomplished a feat, or if he is the first:

> We must also employ many of the means of amplification: for instance, if a man has anything alone (μόνος), or first (πρῶτος), or with a few, or has been chiefly responsible for it: all these circumstances render an action noble. (*Rhet.* 1.9.38)

Amplification also entails praising, or 'making the most' of those acts which are demonstrative of habitual virtue or success:

> Also if a man has often been successful in the same thing: for this is of importance and would appear to be due to the man himself, and not to the result of chance. (*Rhet.* 1.9.38)

Such praise demonstrates that a particular virtuous act was not the result of luck or chance, but resulted from the virtuous and praiseworthy character of the person. Aristotle thirdly encourages the rhetor to amplify a person's praises by noting whether the person has left behind a legacy of praise:

> [We should employ…the means of amplification] if it is for his sake that distinctions which are an encouragement or honour have been invented or established; and if he was the first on whom an encomium was pronounced, as Hippolochus, or to whom a statue was set up in the marketplace, as to Harmodius and Aristogiton. (*Rhet.* 1.9.38)

In other words, a rhetor is taught to accentuate the fact that a person's deeds have had a lasting impact. Deeds become 'more honourable the longer their memory lasts', especially if 'they follow us after death' (*Rhet.* 1.9.25).

Fourthly, the epideictic rhetor was instructed to amplify a person's deeds by comparing him to another illustrious or worthy person:

> And similarly in opposite cases. If he does not furnish you with enough material in himself, you must compare him with others… And you must compare him with illustrious personages (ἐνδόξους), for it affords ground for amplification and is noble, if he can be proved better than men of worth. (*Rhet.* 1.9.40)

Amplification is especially a form of praise, because it has to do with depicting a person's superiority:

> Amplification is with good reason ranked as one of the forms of praise, since it consists in superiority, and superiority (ὑπεροχή) is one of the things that are noble. (*Rhet.* 1.9.39)

Even comparison with an ordinary person was helpful, if it enabled the rhetor to demonstrate the superiority of his subject:

> That is why, if you cannot compare him with illustrious personages, you must compare him with ordinary persons, since superiority is thought to indicate virtue. (*Rhet.* 1.9.38)

Thus, comparison with both illustrious or ordinary persons aided the rhetor in amplifying the praiseworthy superiority of his subjects.

g. *A Rhetoric of Death?*

While the ancient rhetoricians were consistent in their definition of that which made a deed praiseworthy, we are especially interested in the question of whether we may speak of a 'rhetoric of death'. That is to say, did the ancients recognize that certain deaths were honorable, and therefore praiseworthy, while other deaths were shameful, and therefore deserving of blame? Moreover, were there rhetorical guidelines for orators which governed the praise of honorable death?

Aristotle did indeed say that the manner of one's death could be both praiseworthy and noble, or blameworthy and ignoble. In *Nicomachean Ethics,* Aristotle writes: 'The courageous man, therefore, in the proper sense of the term, will be he who fearlessly confronts a noble death' (*Eth. nic.* 3.6.10). If death is met virtuously, that is with righteousness and courage, then it is to be praised accordingly. Conversely, cowardice and disloyalty make a death blameworthy (see *Rhet.* 3.11.8). For Aristotle, dying is by no means a passive event which 'happens' to someone. Death, rather, provides the noble man an opportunity to display virtue and demonstrate his admirability. Aristotle recognizes that one might have to choose between a 'more honourable death' (θάνατος κάλλιον) and an 'expedient life' (τὸ δὲ ζῆν συμφέρον) (*Rhet.* 1.3.6). As such, we should expect that the same rhetorical prescriptions for praising a person in his life may be applied to praising the manner in which a person dies. The rhetor will have as his task to demonstrate that a person died in a praiseworthy manner, befitting his praiseworthy life.

h. *Noble Death in the Rhetoric in Cicero's* De oratore *and Pseudo-Cicero's* Ad Herennium

(1) *The enduring legacy of formal rhetoric.* While Aristotle's *Rhetoric* crystallized the rhetorical conventions of fourth-century Athens, its enduring influence can be seen in such formal rhetorical works as Cicero's *De oratore* and Pseudo-Cicero's *Ad Herennium*. Here we find supporting evidence that the rhetoric of praise found in Aristotle still had resonance in the Greco-Roman world of Luke's own time.

(2) *A rhetoric of death in* Ad Herennium. The author divides honorable behavior into that which is right (*rectum*) and that which is praiseworthy (*laudibile*). Under the category of what is right, the author, like Aristotle, includes all those acts which are 'done in accord with virtue and duty' (*Ad Her.* 3.2.3). Accordingly, it is right (*rectum*) to die in accordance with virtue and duty. The author especially links honorable death to the virtues of courage and justice/righteousness:

> Again, from an honourable act no peril or toil, however great, should divert us; death ought to be preferred to disgrace; no pain should force an abandonment of duty; no man's enmity should be feared in defence of truth; for country, for parents, guest-friends, intimates, and for the things justice commands us to respect, it behooves us to brave any peril and endure any toil. (*Ad Her.* 3.3.5)

Like Aristotle before him, this author defines righteousness as the fulfillment of duty to country and parents. It is better to die honorably for praiseworthy causes than to suffer disgrace.

The author then turns to the topic of praise. That which is praiseworthy 'produces an honorable remembrance, at the time of the event and afterwards' (*Ad Her.* 3.3.7). He treats praise as an inducement to do what is right: 'Indeed, we should pursue the right not alone for the sake of praise; but if praise accrues, the desire to strive after the right is doubled' (3.4.7).

How then might an orator describe death as praiseworthy? The author encourages the rhetor to draw upon rhetorical commonplaces or topoi. For instance, in an argument between doing what is honorable vs. what is safe, the writer argues:

> Virtue ought never to be renounced; either pain, if that is feared, or death, if that is dreaded, is more tolerable than disgrace and infamy; one must consider the shame which will ensue—indeed neither immortality nor a life everlasting is achieved, nor is it proved that once this peril is avoided, another will not be encountered; virtue finds it noble to go even beyond death. (*Ad Her.* 3.5.9)

Pseudo-Cicero contends that pain and death are to be feared less than shame and disgrace. Danger and pain are a price worth paying for the honor which follows.

How then does a noble death fit within the author's discussion of epideictic rhetoric as a whole? He argues that there are three categories of praise: (1) external circumstances, (2) physical attributes, and (3) qualities of character (*Ad Her.* 3.6.10). Under the topic of external circumstances, the rhetor is to address the question, 'What sort of death did he die, and what sort of consequences followed upon it?' (3.7.14). And what is it that makes a death praiseworthy? The author answers:

> In all circumstances, moreover, in which human character is chiefly studied, those four above-mentioned virtues of character [i.e. prudence, justice, courage, and temperance] will have to be applied. Thus, if we speak in praise, we shall say that one act was just, another courageous, another temperate, another wise. (*Ad Her.* 3.7.15)

Like Aristotle before him, the author instructs writers, when praising death, to consider it according to traditional virtue. One may therefore praise a person by demonstrating that he has displayed justice, courage, temperance, and wisdom in facing death.

(3) *The rhetoric of praise in Cicero's* De oratore. Cicero (106–43 BCE) addresses the subject of laudatory rhetoric in, among other places, *De oratore*. Here he offers specific prescriptions for the would-be orator. First, 'laudatory speeches must be delivered occasionally and sometimes written out' (*De orat.* 2.341). Secondly, laudatory rhetoric is a standard tool when dealing with more practical matters: 'These topics of praise and blame (*laudandi et vituperandi*) we shall frequently have occasion to employ in every class of law-suit' (2.349).

How then does an orator go about praising a person? For Cicero, virtue is 'praiseworthy in itself' (*per se ipsa laudabilis*), and 'is a necessary element in anything that can be praised' (2.43). What specific virtues merit praise? Cicero lists the commonplace virtues: 'mercy, justice, kindness, fidelity, courage in common dangers' (2.343). The orator then must demonstrate how these virtues manifest themselves in actions:

> But most welcome praise is that bestowed on deeds that appear to have been performed by brave men without profit or reward; ...for it is virtue that is profitable to others... Also it is customarily recognized as a great and admirable distinction to have borne adversity wisely, not to have been crushed by misfortune, and not to have lost dignity in a difficult situation; and distinction is also conferred by offices filled, rewards of merit

bestowed, and achievements honored by the judgement of mankind; in these matters moreover it is proper to a panegyric to attribute what is merely good fortune to the verdict of divine wisdom. And one must select achievements that are of outstanding importance or unprecedented or unparalleled in their actual character. Moreover, a splendid line to take in panegyric is to compare the subject with other men of high distinction. (*De orat.* 2.346)

As we can see from Cicero's discussion, the commonplaces of formal laudatory rhetoric found in Aristotle are also known, employed, and taught by Cicero. A person is to be praised for being virtuous, and for making the most of his good fortunes (birth, wealth, strength, etc.). Aristotle tells us that victory is praiseworthy. Cicero tells us that the praiseworthy man is not to have been crushed by misfortune. Like Aristotle, Cicero claims that acts are especially praiseworthy if they are done for the sake of others. Likewise, a virtuous deed may be amplified if it is, in some way, unique. Again, like Aristotle, Cicero encourages the orator to amplify praise by means of comparison.

Thus, we see in the rhetorical handbooks that rhetors were expected to touch upon commonplace topics for praise. Especially praiseworthy were deeds performed virtuously. Likewise, a person could be described as praiseworthy if his act was unprecedented and performed in the service of others. Likewise, the noble person would not be crushed or defeated by circumstances. Such commonplaces, as we will see, became a prominent part of the noble death tradition.

3. *Noble Death in Athenian Funeral Speeches*

a. *Introduction to the Funeral Speeches*

A natural avenue into the ancients' understanding of a praiseworthy death is the Athenian funeral speech (ἐπιτάφιος), so named because it was originally delivered graveside.[10] The Athenian funeral speeches provide examples of encomia given in honor of the dead.[11] As such,

10. For the relationship between epideictic literature and the Athenian ἐπιτάφιος, see Theodore Burgesss, *Epideictic Literature* (ed. Leonardo Taran; New York: Garland, 1987), 146-57.

11. The *Progymnasmata* of Theon categorizes the genre of the encomium in this way: 'This encomium, which deals with living persons, is at present specifically called an "encomium", whereas that which deals with the dead is called a "funeral speech", and that which deals with the gods a "hymn". But whether one delivers an encomium about living persons, dead persons, or even heroes or gods, the procedure of these speeches is one and the same' (*Prog.* 9.3-7). See James Butts, 'The Progymnasmata of Theon: A New Text with Translation and Commentary' (unpublished dissertation; Claremont University, CA, 1987).

they allow us to see how the rhetorical rules of Aristotle were applied in praise of those who have died.[12] Extant Athenian funeral speeches include those of Demosthenes, Hyperides, and Lysias, while two others are found in the writings of Thucydides[13] and Plato.[14] While these funeral speeches span the fifth and fourth centuries BCE, their legacy is formidable. Cicero, for instance, tells us that the speech recorded by Plato was read annually in Athens (*De orat.* 2.151). Similarly, Aristotle refers to Lysias's speech in his rhetorical handbook (*Rhet.* 3.10). Pericles' speech furthermore became the standard by which subsequent speeches would be evaluated.

Before proceeding, we should address the context in which these funeral speeches were delivered. According to Thucydides, the Athenians customarily celebrated, at public expense, the funeral rites of those who had died in battle (*History* 2.34.1). The ceremony would take place as follows: (1) the bones of the fallen would lie in state for three days, (2) on the day of the funeral the coffins would be carried to the place of burial, (3) anyone who wished, stranger or citizen, could take part in the procession, (4) the coffins would be laid in a public sepulcher in a beautiful suburb of the city, and (5) women related to the deceased would offer public mourning at the burial site (*History* 2.342-45). What strikes the reader is the very public nature of the ceremony. The funeral rites allowed not only for private grief, but also for the public bestowal of honor. These customs had taken hold by the year 450 BCE, and became annual events,[15] and were soon accompanied by 'contests of strength and knowledge and wealth' (Lysias, *Funeral Oration* 80).[16] The ceremonies culminated with a rhetorical piece written in praise of those who died. For this task, a prominent citizen known for his wisdom and eloquence was chosen to speak.

12. For a thorough assemblage of Athenian funeral topoi, see John E. Ziolkowski, *Thucydides and the Tradition of Funeral Speeches at Athens* (New York: Arno Press, 1981), esp. 93-95.

13. Thucydides (469–401 BCE) records the most famous Athenian funeral speech, *History*, in which Pericles takes for his theme the greatness of Athens.

14. The uniqueness of this *Menexenus*, recorded by Plato (427–347 BCE), is that it is attributed to a certain woman by the name of Aspasia, the Melesian.

15. Isocrates, speaks of the 'annual funerals' (*On the Peace* 87) as does Plato (*Menexenus* 249B).

16. For a detailed discussion concerning the historical origins of the Athenian funeral speech, see Ziolkowski, *Thucydidies and the Tradition of Funeral Speeches*, 13-21.

While the funeral orator was faced with the challenge of presenting an original and meaningful speech, he also had to meet his audience's expectation that certain topics be addressed. As George Kennedy writes:

> The speaker should acknowledge that his words will be inadequate to the occasion; he should praise the ancestors of those who have died by reviewing great moments in the past history of the city; he should offer some consolation to those who are left behind.[17]

The funeral speech was understood by the ancients as a type of forerunner of encomiastic biography. Menander Rhetor tells us that the funeral speech serves two functions: to praise the dead and console the living.[18] The funeral speech differs from the encomium in that it must console those who have lost loved ones to death. However, in its praise of the fallen, it employs the prescriptions of epideictic rhetoric. Indeed, the custom continued for many years, taking on an increasingly encomiastic flavor.[19]As such, the funeral speech was a set rhetorical speech, and was expected to be drawn up according to the rhetorical rules and conventions of the day. Not surprisingly, many modern readers have disparaged Athenian funeral speeches as an 'ossified genre' wholly lacking in originality.[20] However, the rhetorical consistency of these speeches underlines the fact that they transmitted widely accepted cultural values. While the rhetorical handbooks give instruction on how to praise a person, in the Athenian funeral speeches we learn how death specifically is praised. Here, the rhetoric of praise is put into action.[21]

Clearly we see that the funeral speeches follow a set pattern of praise. In reading them, seven motifs clearly emerge as common to the genre. First, the orator typically highlights the courage of those who have died in battle. This is what Pericles calls the 'manly virtue' (ἀνδρὸς ἀρετήν) which enables a soldier to stand his ground rather

17. Kennedy, *A New History of Classical Rhetoric*, 22.

18. See Menander Rhetor, *Treatise* 2.418.

19. As Menander Rhetor notes, 'But because of the passage of time, it has come to be predominantly an encomium (ἐγκώμιον). Who could lament before the Athenians for those who fell 500 years before?' (*Treatise* 2.418).

20. Nicole Loraux defends the originality of the funeral orations, while acknowledging their utilization of many 'topoi', or commonplaces. See, especially, Chapter 5, 'Funeral Oration as Political Genre', in her *The Invention of Athens: The Funeral Oration in the Classical City* (Cambridge, MA: Harvard University Press, 1986).

21. For the thorough assemblage of funeral topoi, see Ziolkowski, *Thucydides and the Tradition of Funeral Speeches*, esp. 93-95.

than flee in the face of danger (Thucydides, *History* 2.42.2). Hyperides praises those who have the 'courage to meet danger gladly' (*Funeral Speech* [hereafter *F.S.*] 37). Likewise, Lysias praises soldiers' fearlessness in the face of 'a multitude of opponents', as they 'exposed their own persons to peril' (*F.S.* 63). For this same reason, Menexenus encourages the parents of the fallen to be brave, as were their sons:

> Moreover, by bearing their calamities thus bravely (ἀνδρείως) they will clearly show that they are in truth the fathers of brave sons and of a like bravery themselves. (*F.S.* 247E)

Time and again the funeral orators praise the courage of those who have fallen in battle.

Secondly, the funeral orators repeatedly praise the fallen for their willingness to die. Demosthenes tells us that the source of honor and glory is 'found in the choice (αἵρεσιν) of those who died nobly' (*F.S.* 37). Indeed, Demosthenes emphasizes that nobility belongs to those who choose death rather than watch their native land fall into misfortune:

> For, since they scorned the love of life that is inborn in all men and chose rather to die nobly (τελευτῆσαι καλῶς μᾶλλον ἠβουλήθησαν) than to live and look upon Greece in misfortune, how can they have failed to leave behind them a record of virtue surpassing all power of words to express? (*F.S.* 19)

Likewise, Pericles exhorts his listeners to follow the example of the dead: 'It is fitting that every man who is left behind should suffer willingly (ἐθέλειν) for her [the city's] sake' (Thucydides, *History* 2.41.5). The fallen are noble because they chose (ἐβουλήθησαν) to fight (2.42.4), and they 'freely sacrificed to her their fairest offering' (2.43.1). Similarly, Lysias makes much of the Athenians' willingness to die. He describes them as 'choosing (αἱρούμενοι) death with freedom rather than life with slavery', and as 'preferring (βουληθέντες) to die in their own land than live to dwell in that of others' (*F.S.* 62). It is this noble choice, made for noble purposes, which makes death praiseworthy:

> Therefore it is fitting to consider those most happy who have closed their lives in risking them for the greatest and noblest ends; not committing their career to chance, nor awaiting the death that comes of itself, but *selecting* the fairest one of all (ἐκλεξάμενοι τὸν κάλλιστον). (*F.S.* 79 [my emphasis])

Menexenus similarly proposes that an ignoble life is a fate worse than death, and therefore the noble man chooses death over dishonor:

> O Children, that ye are born of valiant sires is clearly shown by the facts now before you: we, who might have lived ignobly (μὴ καλῶς) choose rather to die nobly (καλῶς αἱρούμεθα μᾶλλον τελευτᾶν). (*F.S.* 246D)

Thus, willingness and noble choice are important elements in the noble death.

Thirdly, each of the Athenian orators praised the fallen for having died for the sake of others, conferring benefits to others. Lysias, for instance, praises the dead for having brought fame and greatness to their native land:

> For the benefits (αἴτιοι) that they have conferred on their own native land are many and splendid: they restored the broken fortunes of others, and kept the war at a distance from their own country. (*F.S.* 70)

By their deaths, the soldiers 'repaid their native land for their nurture, and, in turn, they earned their city's praise' (*F.S.* 71). By their valor, the fallen had left behind a great legacy to the Athenian people:

> Thus, the Athenian soldiers, through their courageous actions, left behind a legacy of a greater Athens: For we know that they restored in the sight of the world the diminished greatness of our city, revived in her the harmony that had been shattered by faction, and rebuilt walls in place of those that had been demolished. (*F.S.* 63)

Lysias praises not only Athenians but foreigners, who 'came to the support of the people and fought for our salvation (σωτηρίας)' (*F.S.* 66). Similarly, the orator of Plato's *Menexenus* praises the fallen, who 'purchased the safety (σωτηρίας) of the living by their deaths' (*Men.* 237A). Thus, time and again, the orators praise the dead for conferring benefits to others.

Fourthly, the Athenian orators praise the righteousness and virtue of those who have died. *Menexenus* makes this clear when stating the purpose and motivation for his speech: '[And] because of this their valour (ἀρετήν), we pronounce their eulogy now (ἐγκωμιάζονται)' (*Men.* 243D). Lysias, likewise, is concerned to highlight the virtue of those who died. Thus, having recounted the noble ancestry of the fallen dead, Lysias notes that 'in new dangers they brought to memory the ancient virtue of their ancestors (τὴν παλαιὰν ἀρετὴν προγόνων)' (*F.S.* 61). According to Lysias, the Athenian dead 'regarded virtue (ἀρετήν) as their native land, and with this noble end they closed their lives' (66). Lysias tells us that the soldiers 'prized virtue above all else' (71). Again, Pericles praises the fallen who died 'nobly, deeming it their duty (δικαιοῦντες) not to let her be taken from them' (Thucydides, *History* 2.40.5). This duty is clearly in fulfillment of righteousness. Likewise, Demosthenes characterizes the fallen as 'supremely just' (δικαιοτάτοις) (*F.S.* 7). Thus, the orators followed a typical pattern of praising the righteousness and virtue of those who had died.

Fifthly, the Athenian orators accordingly praised the fallen for having died victoriously and unbowed in spirit. Aristotle, we recall, deemed victory praiseworthy, and said that the courageous man would not allow himself to be beaten (*Rhet.* 1.9.24-25). How, then, does one praise a soldier who has been killed in battle? Demosthenes speaks of the victory of those who have fallen:

> Of necessity it happens, when a battle takes place, that the one side is beaten and the other victorious; but I should not hesitate to assert that in my judgement the men who die at the post of duty on either side do not share the defeat but are both alike victors (νικᾶν)... But if, as a mortal being, he meets his doom, what he has suffered is an incident caused by chance, but in spirit he remains unconquered by his opponents (οὐχὶ τὴν ψυχὴν ἥττηται τῶν ἐναντίων). (*F.S.* 19)

Hyperides similarly notes that though Athenian soldiers had lost their lives, their courage resulted in a 'victory gained' (*F.S.* 15). By fulfilling their duties to country, they merit praise for victory.

Sixthly, the orators repeatedly praised the fallen for the uniqueness of what they accomplished. As Aristotle encourages rhetors to praise those who accomplish a certain feat 'first' or 'alone' (*Rhet.* 1.9.38), the Athenian dead are praised for the singularity of their accomplishments. For instance, Plato's *Menexenus* praises Athenian heroes of the past as the 'first and only (μόνη, πρώτη) to produce human nourishment' (*Men.* 237E). Again, the ancestors were the 'first' (πρῶτοι) after the Persian War to help Greeks in behalf of freedom' (242B). Similarly, Demosthenes praises the Athenian soldiers who 'alone' (μόνοι) twice repulsed an Asian army (*F.S.* 10). Lysias likewise praises the Athenian ancestors who were the 'first' (πρῶτοι) and 'only' (μόνοι) to establish democracy (*F.S.* 18). Again, Lysias reminds us that certain fallen soldiers 'alone' (μόνοι) fought for all Greece (*F.S.* 26). Thus, repeatedly the funeral orators praised the unique accomplishments of those who had died.

And finally, the Athenian orators make much of the fact that the Athenian soldiers are worthy of posthumous honors. Among the most obvious of the posthumous honors was the eulogy itself. As Demosthenes notes, 'We ought to honor them with the eulogies as would most certainly secure them in death the glory they had won by living' (*F.S.* 1). In fact, the fame of the fallen would endure for generations. In the words of Lysias, 'Those fallen in war are worthy of receiving the same honours as immortals' (*F.S.* 80). Demosthenes similarly speaks of 'deathless honors' (*F.S.* 33). Such honors, according to Lysias, also included public mourning:

> Hence it is right that the living should yearn for these men and bewail themselves, and pity their kindred for the life that lies before them...for what pleasure now remains for them when such men are being buried. (*F.S.* 71)

Hyperides echoes the thought, claiming that the fallen have merited 'our tears' (*F.S.* 42). *Menexenus* further informs us that posthumous honors included public and private rites held annually, as well as 'contests in athletics and horse-racing and music of every kind' (*Men.* 249B). Demosthenes also speaks of 'sacrifices and games for all future times' (*F.S.* 36). Hymns of praise, likewise, were dedicated to the fallen: 'Already their valour has been adequately celebrated in song by poets who have made it known throughout the world' (*Men.* 239B). Perhaps the most important of the posthumous honors was the public burial itself. Thus, Pericles says, 'In return [for saving Peiraeus] the city has not only mourned them but given them a public funeral, and has granted them in perpetuity the same honours as it gives to its own people' (*History* 2.66). Demosthenes speaks of the burial as an occasion for praise and honor: 'The whole country unites in according them a public burial, and they alone receive the words of universal praise' (*F.S.* 34). Thus, we see that those who died a noble death could expect to receive posthumous honors for generations to come. Their deeds would be remembered and celebrated for generations.

b. *Funeral Speeches: A Summary*

As we have seen the funeral speeches included special praise for (1) courage and (2) willingness to die. Again, the fallen were praised for dying (3) for the sake of others, and (4) in a righteous and virtuous manner. Though they had fallen, they were praised as (5) victorious, and their accomplishments were recognized as (6) unique. As such they were worthy of (7) posthumous honors. These features of praise match closely what we have seen in the formal rhetoric of Aristotle and Cicero. The following chart demonstrates the breakdown of motifs according to each speech. We see that certain themes are clearly commonplace:

Table 1. *Motifs Found in Funeral Speeches*

Motifs	*Thuc.*	*Lysias*	*Plato*	*Demosth.*	*Hyper.*
courage	×	×	×	×	×
willingness	×	×	×	×	×
confers benefits	×	×	×	×	×
righteous	×	×	×	×	
posthumous honors	×	×	×	×	×
unique/ singular	×	×	×	×	×
victory				×	×

As we have seen, the ancients' rhetoric of death has an extensive history, beginning with the funeral speeches and Aristotle and making its way into the Common Era. We will continue to see this rhetoric at work in the progymnasmata and Plutarch's *Lives*.

4. *Noble Death and the Progymnasmata*

a. *Introduction to the Progymnasmata*

The question before us is how the rhetorical conventions of a noble death may have been transmitted to an author such as Luke. Presumably, Luke could have read the rhetorical treatises of Aristotle or the speeches of Thucydides. However, he need not have done so. He would have learned them, most probably, as he learned to write. At the time of Luke, second-level education consisted largely of literary and rhetorical exercises called 'progymnasmata'.[22] It was through the practice of a fixed series of progymnasmatic exercises that a student became mechanically and socially literate. As Matsen, Rollinson, and Sousa write, 'Rhetorical exercises were useful not only for training future public men in the art of speaking persuasively, but also for teaching the fundamentals of literary composition'.[23] As such, the study of rhetoric became nearly coterminous with literacy, and

22. For a discussion of rhetoric's place in the ancients' system of education, see Bonner, *Education in Ancient Rome*, 250-76. Also see Patricia P. Matsen, Philip Rollinson, and Marion Sousa, *Readings from Classical Rhetoric* (Carbondale: Southern Illinois University Press, 1990), 251. See also D.A. Russell, 'Progymnasmata', in *The Oxford Classical Dictionary* (Oxford: Clarendon Press, 2nd edn, 1962), 883.

23. Matsen, Rollinson, and Sousa, *Readings from Classical Rhetoric*, 251.

especially the ability to write.[24] As an author such as Luke learned to write, using the progymnasmata as his textbook, he would have also become familiar with the cultural values embedded in them.

The progymnasmata of Aelius Theon, referenced by the first-century rhetorician Quintilian (35–95 CE) (*Inst.* 3.6.38; 9.3.76), may be dated to the first century BCE. It is thought to be the earliest extant example of the genre.[25] Other extant progymnasmata include those of Hermogenes of Tarsus,[26] Aphthonius,[27] and Nicolaus.[28] Students of the progymnasmata were expected to master any number of written exercises, including the construction of narratives, chreia, maxims, refutations, confirmations, commonplaces, personifications, descriptions, theses, encomia, and comparisons. As Stanley Bonner notes, 'The same subjects recur over the centuries with monotonous regularity'.[29] Yet, this lack of originality served a purpose. The progymnasmata's 'monotonous regularity' preserved and distilled the cultural values of Aristotle's day even to the time of Luke and the centuries which followed.

b. *Encomia: Prescriptions for Praise*

It was particularly through the study of encomia that students learned the rhetorical methods of praise and blame, as well as the cultural values which lay behind them. An encomium was a rhetorical piece written and delivered in honor of a place, thing, or person.[30] Furthermore, the values of the encomia would be reinforced by a

24. See Lucretia Yaghjian's 'Ancient Reading', in Richard Rohrbaugh (ed.), *The Social Sciences and New Testament Interpretation* (Peabody, MA: Hendrickson, 1996), 206-30.

25. Leonard Spengel, *Rhetores Graeci*, II (Leipzig: Teubner, 1854), 112.20.20–115.10; see Butts, 'The Progymnasmata of Theon'.

26. Spengel, *Rhetores Graeci*, II, 14.8–15.5; see C.S. Baldwin, *Medieval Rhetoric and Poetic* (New York: Macmillan, 1928), 23-38.

27. Spengel, *Rhetores Graeci*, II, 42.20–44.19; see Ray Nadeau, 'The Progymnasmata of Aphthonius in Translation', *Speech Monographs* 19 (1952), 264-85.

28. Nicolaus, a sophist, taught rhetoric in Constantinople in the fifth century CE. His work is thought to borrow from Theon. See Matsen, Rollinson, and Sousa, *Readings from Classical Rhetoric*, 263.

29. See Bonner, *Education in Ancient Rome*, 276.

30. Aphthonius summarizes, 'The objects of praise are persons and things, times and places, dumb animals, and, in addition, plants; persons like Thucydides or Demosthenes, things like justice or temperance, times like spring or summer, places like harbors and gardens, dumb animals like a horse or an ox, plants like an olive tree or vine. You may praise in common and singly; in common, as all Athenians, separately, as one Athenian' (Nadeau, 'The Progymnasmata of Aphthonius').

study of synkrisis, or comparison, which, as Kennedy puts it, may be viewed as a 'double encomium'.[31] Admittedly, the encomia have little to say specifically about the act of dying.[32] Theon, however, informs us that the encomium is part of the same genre as that of the funeral speech:

> This encomium deals with living persons, is at present specifically called an encomium (ἐγκώμιον), whereas that which deals with the dead is called a funeral speech (ἐπιτάφος), and that which deals with the gods a hymn (ὕμνος). But whether one delivers an encomium about living persons, dead persons, or even heroes or gods, the procedure of the speeches is one and the same. (*Prog.* 9.4-8)

As the funeral speech and the encomium fall into the same genre, the rules for praising a person's life will tell us much about how to praise his death.

What, according to the encomia, are some of the characteristics of noble actions? What makes an action particularly praiseworthy? As Aristotle and the funeral orators praised those who died virtuously, Theon writes, 'Virtue shines forth especially in misfortunes' (*Prog.* 9.74). Again, the funeral orators praised the fallen for their courage. Aristotle defines courage in this way: 'It makes men perform noble acts in the midst of danger' (*Rhet.* 1.9.7). So also, Theon praises the courage of those who take on 'dangers for the sake of friends' (*Prog.* 9.34). As Aristotle and the funeral orators praised those who remained unconquered in spirit, Theon offers his students this advice: 'If he has none of the aforementioned good qualities [i.e. good fortune], one must say that although he met with misfortune he was not humbled' (9.65-67). Theon praises those who are not humbled by misfortune or made slavish when facing difficult circumstances.

Following rhetorical convention, Theon predicates the nobility of an action upon its benefit to others. Accordingly, an act is praiseworthy if it is done 'for the sake of others' (ἄλλων ἕνεκα) (*Prog.* 9.29). An action is especially praiseworthy if 'the benefit is shared; and on account of which most people also receive great benefits' (9.31-32). One should praise the person who eschews what is 'pleasant' or

31. Kennedy, *A New History of Classical Rhetoric*, 205.

32. He does include εὐθανασία, as a quality to be praised. As a noun, the term may refer to a noble death (see Cicero, *Atticus* 16.7.3). Likewise, the verb εὐθανατέω can refer to dying nobly (*SVF* 3.156; Polybius 5.38.9). Yet, since the term εὐθανασία appears in Theon under the heading of 'external qualities', it likely may refer simply to an easy or 'happy death', that is, one without diminishment or pain.

'advantageous' to himself and 'takes on hardship for the benefit of others' (9.30-32).

According to Aristotle and the funeral orators, a person was especially laudable if he was the first or only person to accomplish a specific feat. Theon echoes this sentiment:

> Praiseworthy actions are also those occurring in a timely manner, and if one acted alone (μόνος), or first (πρῶτος), or when no one acted, or more than others, or with a few, or beyond one's age, or exceeding expectation, or with hard work, or what was done most easily and quickly. (*Prog.* 9.35-38)

By demonstrating that someone acted first or alone, the rhetor will demonstrate that a person's accomplishments stand out from the deeds of others.

Again, according to Aristotle, actions are 'more honourable the longer their memory lasts' (*Rhet.* 1.9.25). Funeral orators claimed that the fallen were worthy of posthumous honors. Likewise, Theon notes that noble actions are 'those which are applauded after death (μετὰ θάνατον)' (*Prog.* 9.25). In each case, honor lives beyond the grave.

Thus, we see in Theon, as in Aristotle and the funeral speeches, that the noble death (1) will be characterized by virtues, especially courage, (2) will confer benefits to others, (3) will be singular and unique, and (4) will be rewarded with posthumous honors. In Theon, we see a good summary of the all that makes a life and death praiseworthy.

c. *Vituperation: Blaming a Shameful Death*

While none of the extant progymnasmata offer a specific prescriptive example of how to praise a noble death, the *Progymnasmata* of Aphthonius offers an example of its opposite in 'A Vituperation of Philip'. A vituperation is, by definition, an encomium's opposite:

> It is divided into the same topics as the encomium, and it is required to find fault with just as many things as are objects of praise... And in making a beginning, you will bring forth the genus, which you will divide in the same way as the encomium, and you will set down the education, the achievements, the comparison, and the epilogue, just as in encomia. (*Progymnasmata* 275)

Aphthonius writes that 'it is fitting to tell about the death' of Philip in that it gives evidence of his shameful life. Aphthonius writes:

> But it is also fitting to tell about the death of this man. For, as he subjected everything to himself as he advanced and through treachery enslaved those who made treaties with him, the gods, in anger because of the broken treaties, brought a death appropriate to him. For they did not destroy him in battle, nor did they make heroism a witness to his death, but they

> put an end to him amid nothing but worldly pleasures, thus making pleasure a shroud worthy of the evil deeds of Philip, so that both in life and in death he might have witness to his incontinence. (*Progymnasmata* 276)

Shame is the appropriate reward for the one who acts treacherously and lives apart from virtue. Further, a shameful death is unaccompanied by heroism, and marked by the vices of intemperance and lack of self-control. Aphthonius describes Philip's deeds as being self-serving acts of 'incontinence'. This contrasts with the noble death, in which a person acts for the sake of others. Again, Philip's death is characterized by its unrighteousness.

d. *Summary of Noble Death in the Progymnasmata*

From the progymnasmata, students studied those things which society prized. They also learned certain categories for praising individuals. We see that the rhetorical criteria for praising a person's death in Aristotle (formal rhetoric), the funeral orations (rhetoric in practice), and the progymnasmata (educational rhetoric) were common, constant, and conventional. The progymnasmata distill centuries-old values. They teach that the noble death is characterized by virtue, especially courage. The noble person dies willingly, and for the sake of others. Likewise, the noble person will die righteously, in accordance with his duties to god, country, and ancestors. As Aristotle claimed that victory was noble, Theon tells us that the noble person is not humbled or made slavish by outward circumstances. Again dispensing age-old rhetorical wisdom, Theon deems praiseworthy those acts which are singular, because the person performs the act first, alone, or under especially difficult circumstances.

5. *The Rhetoric of Death in Plutarch's* Lives

a. *Introduction to Plutarch's* Lives

Plutarch (46–126 CE), a contemporary of Luke, produced voluminous writings including the *Moralia*, in which he dispenses wisdom on moral and ethical principles. However, the author is most celebrated for his *Lives*, in which he compares and contrasts famous public figures of Greece and Rome.

There has been some debate as to whether Plutarch's *Lives* conform more closely to the genre of history or biography.[33] In his accounts of

33. D.A. Russell, *On Reading Plutarch's Lives* (Berkeley: University of California Press, 1974), 87, argues that Plutarch's *Lives* lack such basic elements of history as 'speeches, battles, geographical excursuses', but acknowledges that

Romulus and Theseus, Plutarch says that he aims to purify their stories from the elements of fable, and arrive at the 'semblance of history' (ἱστορίας ὄψιν) (*Thes.* 1.3). At the same time, Plutarch claims, 'It is not Histories that I am writing, but Lives; and in the most illustrious deeds there is not always a manifestation of virtue or vice' (*Alex.* 1.2). Yet, whether they are closer to history or biography, his *Lives* do have a pronounced rhetorical flavor. In this, Plutarch is heir of the Greek tradition of encomiastic biography, which has its roots in the writings of Plato and Xenophon.[34]

First of all, we should note that the very structure of Plutarch's *Lives* is drawn from formal rhetoric. Following a typical rhetorical pattern, Plutarch tells of the 'life' of a Greek orator, soldier, or politician, and follows it with the story of a comparable Roman. Many of the topics which Plutarch touches upon in his *Lives* are based upon the standard elements of the encomium. He then concludes with a comparison of the two. Clearly, in his use of comparison, Plutarch is indebted to his rhetorical training.[35]

Secondly, the standards by which Plutarch judges the character of his subjects are largely those found in encomia. Accordingly, concerning each of Plutarch's subjects, we likely will be told about his noble (or common) lineage,[36] his nurture and training,[37] deeds of the body,[38] deeds of the soul,[39] and deeds of fortune.[40]

they are 'based on history'. R.H. Barrow (*Plutarch and his Times* [Bloomington: Indiana University Press, 1967], 57) notices the same things, and notes that Plutarch 'does in fact include much history in his *Lives*'. C.J. Giankaris dismisses the distinction between biography and history by equating the two, noting, 'In previous eras history *was* biography'. See Giankaris, *Plutarch* (New York: Twayne Publishers, 1970), 38.

34. See Arnaldo Momigliano, *Development of Greek Biography* (Cambridge, MA: Harvard University Press, 1971); also Patricia Cox, *Development of Greek Biography* (Berkeley: University of California Press, 1983).

35. George Kennedy, noting the indebtedness of first-century writers to progymnastic compositional building-blocks, writes, 'Among Greek writers of the First Century, Dio Chrysostom probably best exemplifies the adaptation of progymnasmata to extended composition, but the *Parallel Lives* of Plutarch contain the most famous examples of *synkriseis*' (*Greek Rhetoric*, 56).

36. See, among many examples: Alcibiades, whose family 'may be traced back to Eurysaces' (*Alc.* 1.1); or Sulla, who 'belonged to a patrician or noble family' (*Sull.* 1.1); or Cleander, who was 'a man of the highest lineage' (*Phil.* 1.1). If some supernatural phenomenon occurred during birth, this was also recorded. For instance, a phantom (φάσμα) appeared and predicted Cicero would be 'a great blessing to all Romans' (*Cic.* 1.2).

37. Of Alexander, we are told that he received the finest training from a group of 'nurturers, tutors, and teachers', most especially from 'Leonidas, a man

For Plutarch, the way in which a person dies often makes the difference in judging the character of an entire life. According to Plutarch, neither life nor death matters as much as 'the accomplishment of them both with honour' (*Pel.* 1.4). The standards by which Plutarch judges a death noble or ignoble are largely those inculcated through rhetorical training and education.[41] Plutarch writes of the relative merits of Agis, Cleomenes, and the Gracchi, 'I think, too, that the way in which the men died makes a difference in their high excellence' (*Comp. Ag. Cleom. cum Ti. Gracch.* 3.1). An exemplary death culminates a life of achievement and virtue.[42] Conversely, a death poorly faced could put a 'stain' on one's life (*Eum.* 2.4). Even more, the manner of one's death could do much to redeem an ignoble life, as in the case of Cato the Younger, whose record of indiscretions 'was blotted out and removed by the manner of his death' (*Cat. Min.* 73.3). Likewise, we think of Otho, who, 'though he lived no more decently than Nero, he died more nobly (ἀπέθανεν εὐγενέστερον)' (*Oth.* 18.2).

Commenting on Plutarch's indebtedness to rhetorical composition, Philip Shuler classifies the *Lives* as laudatory biography, and adds,

of stern temperament' (*Alex.* 5.4). Cicero's education was exemplary, and he showed himself 'fond of learning and fond of wisdom, capable of welcoming all knowledge' (*Cic.* 2.2). Cato the Younger had the benefit of having as a tutor, 'a man of culture' (*Cat. Min.* 1.3).

38. Plutarch often comments on his subjects' comeliness. Concerning Pompey, we are told that his 'boyish loveliness had a gentle dignity about it, and in the prime and flower of his youthful beauty, there was at once manifest the majesty and kingliness of his nature' (*Pomp.* 2.1). Plutarch waxes poetic about Alcibiades, whose 'beauty... flowered out with each successive season of his bodily growth' (*Alc.* 1.3; see also *Ti. C. Gracch.* 2.1; *Sull.* 1.2). Plutarch also tells us, when appropriate, of his subjects' bodily strength. Of Aratus, we informed of 'high health and stature' and 'athletic look', which resulted in winning wreaths in the pentathlon (*Arat.* 2.3).

39. Plutarch judges his subjects according to the commonplace virtues taught in rhetorical composition: justice, courage, wisdom, temperance, and the like. Alexander, Lysander, Pompey, and Coriolanus are praised for their 'self-restraint' (σωφροσύνη) (*Alex.* 4.4; *Comp. Lys. Sull.* 5.5; *Pomp.* 1.3; *Comp. Alc. Cor.* 5.2); Phocion is praised for rushing into battle with boldness (θυμῷ) (*Phoc.* 6.1); Sulla is commended for courage (ἀνδρείας) (*Comp. Lys. Sull.* 5.5). Nicias is praised for exercising the tools of a wise leader (ἡνεμένος ἔμφρονος) (*Comp. Nic. Crass.* 4.1). Other examples abound.

40. Deeds of fortune include power, wealth, friends, children, fame, length of life, and a happy (easy) death (Theon, *Prog.* 9).

41. Alan Wardman reminds us not to overlook Plutarch's rhetorical education. See *Plutarch's Lives* (Berkeley: University of California Press, 1974), 221-24.

42. See, for instance, *Ag. and Cleom.* 37.6.

'Its aims were closely associated, if not identical with, the intent and purposes of epideictic oratory as described by the rhetoricians'.[43] Shuler may overstate the case. Surely, Plutarch remains both a historian and moral philosopher. That being said, the 'intellectual equipment' of the encomiast and the biographer are, in Wardman's words, 'not much different'.[44] Plutarch is a biographer/historian/moralist who draws upon his rhetorical training to evaluate and present the nobility or ignobility of the people he depicts. One of the ways he does this is to describe a death as noble or ignoble. Thus, as we study Plutarch's *Lives*, we move from the field of epideictic oratory, strictly speaking, to a broader field of biography, colored by epideictic rhetoric.[45]

b. *Noble Death Characterized by Courage*

According to Plutarch, a good death is one met with courage and valor. The courageous man is willing to face danger, as in the case of Brutus, who 'risked danger (προεκινδύνευεν)', which 'redounds to [his] praise (ἔπαινον)' (*Comp. Dion. Brut.* 2.4). Cato the Younger developed a reputation as a philanderer, but gained honor through his courageous death:

> But all such ill-report was blotted out and removed by the manner of his death. For he fought at Philippi against Caesar and Antony, in behalf of liberty; and when his line of battle was giving way, he deigned not either to fly or to hide himself, but challenged the enemy, displayed himself in front of them, cheered on those who held their ground with him, and so fell, after amazing his foes by his valour (ἀρετῆς). (*Cat. Min.* 73.3; see *Comp. Pel. Marc.* 3.2)

Courage does not belong to the soldier alone. Cratesicleia, the wife of Panteus, receives special praise for the way she 'bravely (ἡρωϊκῶς) met her end' (*Ag. Cleom.* 38.6). Indeed, '[she] was not one whit dismayed by death, but asked one favor only, that she might die before the children died' (38.4).

The courageous man will remain calm in the face of death. Aristotle prescribed praise for those who remained 'stout-hearted in adversity' (*Rhet.* 1.9.31), a prescription echoed by Theon: 'Virtue shines forth especially in misfortune' (*Prog.* 9.76). Similarly, Plutarch accords special praise to those who meet death with equanimity, not

43. Philip Shuler, *A Genre for the Gospels: The Biographical Character of Matthew* (Philadelphia: Fortress Press, 1982), 56.

44. Wardman, *Plutarch's Lives*, 242.

45. For a discussion of the transition from epideictic oratory to the use of epideictic oratory in history/biography, see Burgess, *Epideictic Literature*.

succumbing to such emotions as grief or fear. As Alan Wardman writes, 'His general position is not that the passions should be entirely eliminated, but that they should be moderated'.[46] What matters for Plutarch is not the presence or absence of the passions, but the ability to remain level-headed, and do the right thing. For, while fortune may succeed in bringing evils, it 'cannot rob virtue of the power to endure those evils with calm assurance' (*Caius Gracch.* 19.3). Accordingly, we are told that while his friends were overcome with grief at his imminent execution, 'the countenance of Phocion was the same as it used to be when he was escorted from the assembly as a general, and when men saw it, they were amazed by the man's calmness (ἀπάθειαν), and at his grandeur of spirit' (*Phoc.* 36.1). Similarly, Pompey receives high praise for submitting to death in a calm and dignified manner:

> And Pompey, drawing his toga down over his face with both hands, without an act or word that was unworthy of himself, with a groan merely, submitted to their blows. (*Pomp.* 79.4)

This noble tranquility is illustrated well in Plutarch's account of Otho, who, on the night before his death, 'slept so soundly that his chamberlains heard his heavy breathing' (*Oth.* 17.2). Far from being overcome by sorrow or grief, the noble man often comforts those around him (see *Oth.* 17.1-2).

c. *Noble Death Characterized by Righteousness*

As seen above, Pseudo-Aristotle deemed righteousness praiseworthy, and further defined the virtue according to its parts: the fulfilling of one's duties to the gods, country, and parents/ancestors (*Virt. Vit.* 5.2-4). Likewise, Plutarch offered praise for those who had died righteously. For Plutarch, the fallen are worthy of praise if they have done what they ought to have done, especially in regard to the gods, to their country, and to their parents/ancestors.

Chief among the duties of righteousness is piety towards the gods. The pious man is both god-loving and god-loved.[47] In order to demonstrate a person's nobility, Plutarch will often recount acts of piety (εὐσέβεια) in the face of death. These acts of piety include offering sacrifices to the gods. For instance, Plutarch tells us that when Themistocles wanted to put a 'fitting end' to his life, he 'made a sacrifice to the gods' (*Them.* 21.5). Similarly, we are told that Alexander performed his customary religious duties, even in his dying days:

46. Wardman, *Plutarch's Lives*, 108.
47. See Menander Rhetor, *Treatise* 1.361.20-25.

> Then when it was late, he took a bath, performed his sacrifices to the gods (τὰ ἱερὰ τοῖς θεοῖς), ate a little, and had a fever through the night. On the twentieth, after bathing again, he performed the customary sacrifice (ἔθυσε τὴν εἰθισμένην θυσίαν). (*Alex*. 76.2)

Likewise, Aemilius Paulus is praised for fulfilling his religious duties in his dying days. Aemilius offered 'public sacrifice', and on the next day 'sacrificed again to the gods privately in gratitude for his recovery' (*Aem*. 39.2). Three days later Aemilius died, and Plutarch pronounced him 'fully blessed with everything that men think conducive to happiness' (*Aem*. 39.3). Again, Galba is praised for his pious desire 'to sacrifice to Jupiter' (*Galb*. 26.2). In each of the above examples, the righteous person is one who performs religious services to the gods.

The person who is pious towards the gods, is also loved by them, as was Demosthenes, whose death was not due to poison, but 'to the honor and kindly favour shown by the gods, that he was rescued from the cruelty of the Macedonians by a speedy and painless death' (*Dem*. 77).

As we noted in the funeral speeches, duty to one's country was a featured component of righteousness and, as such, was grounds for praise. We see this also in Plutarch's *Lives*. The author judges a person's life noble if it is offered for the sake of one's homeland. Thus Marcellus, who died in battle, is honored for being a 'great star of his country, Rome' (*Marc*. 30.5). Galba is praised for offering his life for the good of the people:

> The soldiers ran up and struck at him. Yet, he merely presented his neck to their swords, saying: 'Do your work, if this is better for the Roman people'. (*Galb*. 27.2)

Dion, likewise, is praised for hazarding a peril so great 'in order to save Sicily' (*Comp. Dion. Brut*. 1.3). Brutus is praised because he 'risked his life for the common liberty (τῆς κοινῆς ἐλευθερίας)' (*Comp. Dion. Brut*. 2.4).

Plutarch also praises some for the virtue of filial piety. For instance, he lauds Demetrius for being a father-lover (φιλοπάτωρ), who looked after his mother and honored his father (*Demetr*. 3.1).

d. *Noble Death Faced Willingly*

For Plutarch, the unseemly desire to escape death signals shamefulness and cowardice. Conversely, to accept death willingly is a sign of nobility. Plutarch writes:

> I think, too that the way in which the men died makes a difference in their high excellence. For the Gracchi fought against their fellow citizens, and then died as they sought to escape; but in the case of the Greeks, Agis would not kill a single citizen, and therefore died what one might almost call a voluntary death (ἑκὼν ἀπέθανε), and Clemonenes, after setting out to avenge himself for insults and wrongs, found the occasion unfavorable and with good courage slew himself. (*Comp. Ag. Cleom. cum Ti. Gracch.* 3.1)

This does not mean that Plutarch judges all voluntary deaths to be noble. For instance, 'it is no great thing' to seek death if it is merely to 'escape hardship' (*Pel.* 1.3). Accordingly, Plutarch has no praise for the younger Marius, who was imprisoned for his cruelty, and killed himself after many vain attempts to escape (*Mar.* 66.6). In such a case, Marius was not so much willing to die, as he was unwilling to endure hardship. Most shameful is the death of one who seeks, at the cost of honor, to flee:

> Nicias was led by the hope of a shameful and inglorious safety to put himself into the hands of his enemies, thereby making his death a greater disgrace for him. (*Comp. Nic. Crass.* 5.2)

e. *Noble Death is Met on One's Own Terms (Not as a Victim)*

Aristotle tells us that victory is honorable, and defeat ignoble. The funeral speeches tell us that even the fallen are not beaten if they fight with courage until the end. Similarly, Plutarch especially praises those who exhibit control of their own destiny and willingly face the death which lies ahead of them.

Thus, Plutarch favorably quotes Cato the Younger, who, before taking his own life, declared, 'I must be the master of the course I decide to take' (*Cat. Min.* 69.3). Likewise, Anthony's death, while cowardly, was made more honorable by the fact that he died before 'his enemy became master of his person' (*Comp. Demetr. Ant.* 6.2). It was possible to retain mastery of the situation, even in the face of outward humiliation. For instance, Phocion's 'grandeur of spirit' is displayed in his calm self-assurance in the face of his enemies' insults:

> His enemies, however, ran along by his side and reviled him; and some of them actually came up and spat in his face. At this we are told, Phocion looked towards the magistrates and said, 'Will not someone stop this fellow's unseemly behavior'. (*Phoc.* 36.2)

Phocion, though physically a slave, remained the master of his circumstances. By speaking authoritatively, Phocion offers an example of what the ancients deemed 'bold speech' (παρρησία), which is a virtuous frankness born of courage. Phocion, though outwardly defeated, remained unbowed.

Conversely, Eumenes' death is judged deficient because he allowed himself to become a victim:

> Eumenes, however, who was unable to fly before being taken prisoner, but was willing to live after being taken prisoner, neither took good precautions against death, nor faced it well, but by supplicating and entreating the foe who was known to have power over his body only, he made him lord and master of his spirit also. (*Comp. Eum. Sert.* 1.3)

Eumenes saved his life, but lost his honor.

f. *Noble Death is for the Sake of Others*

Rhetorical convention esteems deeds more noble when performed for the sake of others (cf. Aristotle, *Rhet.* 1.9.23; Theon, *Prog.* 9.30). Thus, the emperor Otho, seeing his death as redemption for misspent years, pleads, 'But do not rob me of the greater blessedness—that of dying nobly in behalf of fellow citizens so many and so good' (*Oth.* 15.4; cf. 17.3). Similarly, Pelopidas is praised for dying 'in defence of the freedom of Thessaly' (*Pel.* 34.5). Indeed, he encouraged the soldiers under his leadership to 'risk their lives' for the sake of their 'native city' (*Pel.* 7.1-2). Plutarch time and again praises those who died for the sake of their country (cf. *Arist.* 26.1; *Cim.* 19.1).

g. *The Uniqueness of One's Accomplishments*

In praise of his subjects, Plutarch employs techniques of amplification; for instance, he praises his subjects if they are chiefly responsible for some great accomplishment, or have been the first or only person to do something (see Aristotle, *Rhet.* 1.9.38). Thus, Plutarch praises Pericles as being chiefly responsible for the building of sacred buildings, including the Parthenon. Plutarch writes, 'Each of them [the temples], men thought, would require many successive generations to complete it, but all of them were completed in the heyday of a single administration (μιᾶς ἀκμῇ πολιτείας)' (*Per.* 12.1; see also *Comp. Per. Fab.* 2.5). Likewise, Plutarch praises Timoleon especially because he as commander was chiefly responsible for his military victories, which he achieved despite leading a poor army: 'For when equal successes follow an unequal equipment, greater credit (αἰτίαν) accrues to the commander' (*Comp. Tim. Aem.* 1.2). Again, we are told that Publica was chiefly responsible for his country's successes, 'for he saw his country victorious through his efforts as consul and general' (*Comp. Sol. Publ.* 1.3). Again, Plutarch praises Numa, who alone changed a city not yet in sympathy with his views, and who, 'by his wisdom and justice won the hearts of all the citizens and brought them into harmony' (*Comp. Lyc. Num.* 4.8). Likewise, Timoleon is praised not only for his justice and probity in the administration of his affairs, but also because he alone acted justly in the midst of corruption: 'Of the Greek leaders and generals who took part in Sicilian affairs during the time of Timoleon, not one was free from corruption except Dion' (*Comp. Aem. Tim.* 2.1).

Similarly, Plutarch praises Romulus, because only three Roman generals achieved the honor of killing the opposing general in battle, and, of the three, he was the first (πρώτῳ) (*Rom.* 16.7). Likewise, Lycurgus is praised for being the *first* to introduce many new things. Included among his many innovations (πλειόνων καινοτομουμένων), 'the first and foremost was his institution of a senate', which 'brought safety and due moderation into counsels of state' (*Lyc.* 5.6).

h. *Noble Death is accompanied by Posthumous Honors: Public Mourning, Praise, an Appropriate Burial, and Special Dedications*

According to Aristotle, the epideictic rhetor is to praise 'those things which follow us after death' (*Rhet.* 1.9.25). The progymnasmata also offers as praiseworthy those actions which 'are applauded after death' (*Prog.* 9.25). For Plutarch, too, a person's greatness can be seen not only in his own actions, but in the manner in which people mourn his death.

In Plutarch's *Lives*, the death of a noble man is rightfully accompanied by grief and lament. Public mourning signifies not only sadness, but also a bestowal of honor. Desirous of such honor, Solon pleads, 'May not an unlamented (ἄκλαυστος) death be mine, but unto friends let me be cause, when dead, for sorrow (ἄλγεα) and for sighing (στοναχάς)' (*Comp. Sol. Publ.* 1.4). Such public grief made Publicola a blessed man (εὐδαίμονα):

> For when he died, his loss filled not only friends and kindred, but the entire city, numbering tens of thousands, with weeping and yearning and sorrow. For the women of Rome mourned for him as though they had lost a son, or a brother, or a common father. (*Comp. Sol. Publ.* 1.4)

Numa, we are told, was to be envied for a burial which included a procession in which 'the people, including women and children, followed with groans and lamentations' (*Num.* 22.1). Publicola brought his life to perfection 'with a mourning that was honourable and enviable' (*Publ.* 23.3). Conversely, an ignoble man's death brings either joy or indifference. Thus, when Caius Marius died, 'Rome was filled with great rejoicing' (*Mar.* 46.5).

Public mourning also entailed praise of the fallen. Nowhere is this better evidenced than in the death of Pelopidas, whom his fellow

Thebans called their 'father, savior, and teacher of the greatest and fairest blessings' (*Pel.* 33.1).

Throughout his *Lives*, Plutarch further accentuates the nobility of his subjects by telling of their honorable burials. For the ancients, the burial of a great man was considered a 'pious privilege' (*Pomp.* 80.3). For instance, Phocion, at his death, received a lowly, private burial by his pious wife (*Phoc.* 37.3). Yet, when the people realized what a great man they had lost, 'they set up a statue of him in bronze, and gave his bones a public burial' (*Phoc.* 38.1).[48] Of Philopoemen we are told, 'He was buried, then, as was fitting, with conspicuous honors' (*Phil.* 21.5). Likewise, Timandra honored her husband Alcibiades by giving him as 'brilliant and honourable burial as she could provide' (*Alc.* 39.5). Again, Caesar showed his admiration for Cleopatra's 'lofty spirit' by ordering 'that her body should be buried with that of Anthony in splendid and regal fashion' (*Ant.* 86.4).

One particular way to honor the fallen was the provision for spices for the deceased. Plutarch favorably notes that for the funeral of Sulla, women contributed a 'vast quantity of spices' (*Sull.* 38.2). Similarly, we are told that Demetrius's body was treated with 'garlands and other honours' (*Demetr.* 53.3). Treatment of the body with spices and garlands served as a means to show both respect and honor for the fallen.

Often, the ancients would dedicate memorial statues and buildings to honor the dead. Plutarch offers a number of such examples. For instance, the Athenians honored Demosthenes by 'erecting his statue in bronze' (*Dem.* 30.5). Marcellus' memory was preserved by the dedication of 'a gymnasium at Catina in Sicily, and statues and paintings from the treasures of Syracuse' (*Marc.* 30.4).

Plutarch also makes the point that in certain cases, the gods are said to honor the fallen through special, supernatural occurrences. For instance, the tomb of Lycurgus is said to have been struck by lightning, testimony to the fact that he was 'holy and beloved of the gods (θεοφιλεστάτῳ)' (*Lyc.* 31.3). In this light, we may also consider the case of Romulus. At his death, Plutarch reports, 'the light of the sun was eclipsed' (*Rom.* 27.6). Likewise, in his account of Caesar's death, we are told that there was an 'obscuration of the sun's rays', which caused the sun to shine with less light and heat for a year (*Caes.* 69.4). This sign, among others, showed that 'the murder of Caesar was not pleasing to the gods' (*Caes.* 69.5).

48. Aristotle includes the dedication of a statue as a means for amplifying praise (*Rhet.* 1.9.38).

6. *A Summary of Noble Death Motifs*

At this time it may prove helpful to review the basic motifs of the noble and praiseworthy death, as seen in Formal Rhetoric (Aristotle, Pseudo-Cicero, and Cicero), the Funeral Orations, Educational Rhetoric (Theon), and Plutarch's *Lives*. The following chart summarizes our findings thus far:

Table 2. *A Summary of Noble Death Motifs*

Motifs	*Aristotle*	*Funeral Speech*	*Progymnasmata*	*Plutarch's Lives*
courage	×	×	×	×
Righteousness	×	×	×	×
willingness	×	×	×	×
victory	×	(not a victim)	(not humbled)	(not a victim)
Benefits others	×	×	×	×
Unique/ Timely	×	×	×	×
Posthumous honors	×	×	×	×

As shown above, there is in our sources near unanimity on the essential features of what makes a death noble and praiseworthy. This tradition clearly enjoyed a long and broad history. The motifs of the noble death are evident from the time of the Athenian funeral speeches. These same motifs are taught by the likes of Aristotle and Cicero. Furthermore, authors contemporary to Luke, such as Plutarch, made use of these motifs in their writing of history. The values of a praiseworthy death were transmitted via the study of progymnasmata, and, as such, would have been familiar to those who demonstrated literacy. The ancient writers, trained in rhetoric and absorbed in its culture, knew and used common motifs for describing a person's death as honorable and praiseworthy.

7. *Rhetoric and Luke*

a. *Rhetorical Elements in Luke–Acts*

With Plutarch's *Lives*, we have seen an example of a historian/biographer who was able to draw upon his knowledge of rhetoric and, more particularly, the basic elements of epideictic rhetoric, to assess and depict the praiseworthy/blameworthy aspects of a person's death. So also, with Luke, we have an example of a historian who was trained in rhetorical composition. Like Plutarch, Luke was well educated and versed in the culture of the Greco-Roman world.

For a number of years, the Gospels were thought to be more the product of oral transmission than rhetorical composition. Within recent years, however, the Gospels have been recognized as products of a rhetorical culture in which oral and written speech interacted closely.[49] This recognition has led scholars to see that the Gospels, much like Plutarch's *Lives*, are products of rhetorically trained writers.[50]

Luke–Acts offer us ample evidence of Luke's skill as a writer, and his knowledge of Greco-Roman rhetorical and literary conventions.[51] Luke opens both Luke and Acts with highly stylized historical prefaces (Lk. 1.1-4; Acts 1.1-5).[52] Furthermore, Luke uses these prefaces to bind his two books together, making use of the literary technique of recapitulation and resumption, a technique used by Polybius, Strabo, Diodorus, Josephus, and Herodian.[53] Luke opens Acts with a recapitulation of the first book: 'In the first book, O Theophilus, I have dealt with all that Jesus began to do and teach'. Luke then proceeds to resume the story by retelling the conclusion of Luke (Lk. 24.36-53; Acts 1.2-5). By his employment of literary prefaces, Luke shows

49. See T.M. Lentz, *Orality and Literacy in Hellenic Culture* (Carbondale: Southern Illinois University Press, 1989).

50. See Vernon K. Robbins, 'Writing as a Rhetorical Act in Plutarch and the Gospels', in Duanne Watson (ed.), *Persuasive Artistry: Studies in New Testament Rhetoric in Honor of George A. Kennedy* (JSNTSup, 50; Sheffield: JSOT Press, 1991), 157-86.

51. For a discussion of Luke's knowledge of rhetorical handbooks, see Mikeal C. Parsons, 'Luke and the *Progymnasmata*: A Preliminary Investigation into the Preliminary Exercises', in Todd Penner and Caroline Vander Stichele (eds.), *Contextualizing Acts: Lukan Narrative and Greco-Roman Discourse* (SBLSP, 20; Atlanta: Society of Biblical Literature, 2003), 43-65.

52. The Lukan prefaces are commonly compared with the historical prefaces of Herodotus, Thucydides, and Polybius, as well as with prefaces of treatises by such Hellenistic Jewish authors as Aristeas and Josephus. See Gregory Sterling, *Historiography and Self Definition* (Leiden: E.J. Brill, 1992), 339-46; as well as Vernon K. Robbins, 'Prefaces in Greco-Roman Biography and Luke–Acts', in Paul Achtemeier (ed.), *Society of Biblical Literature 1978 Seminar Papers* (Missoula, MT: Scholars Press, 1978), 193-207. For further discussion of Luke's place among Greek historians, see L.C.A. Alexander's 'Luke's Preface in the Context of Greek Preface-Writing', *NovT* 28.1 (1986), 48-74, and her more recent 'The Preface of Acts and the Historians', in Ben Witherington, III (ed.), *History, Literature, and Society in the Book of Acts* (Cambridge: Cambridge University Press, 1996), 73-103.

53. See Aune, *The New Testament*, 117-18.

himself to be not only a historian, but a rhetor, capable of highly refined writing. As Arthur Just remarks, Luke's prologue, framed as a 'brilliant periodic sentence' surely 'would impress a Hellenistic audience'.[54] Erhardt Güttgemans notes that the Lukan preface contains five (possibly eight) technical rhetorical terms, and that therefore the work should be considered 'rhetorical', as opposed to 'historical'.[55]

Güttgemans's claim creates an unnecessary chasm between history and rhetoric, but does draw our attention to Luke's rhetorical skills. Luke's ability as historian and rhetorician is also seen in his composition of speeches, of which some thirty are included in the book of Acts. These speeches, through which Luke portrays his characters, demonstrate his knowledge of προσωποιΐα and ἠθοποιΐα, standard headings in the progymnasmata.[56] A number of these speeches may be classified as defense speeches, a common rhetorical type.[57] The writing of speeches was among the skills learned in the progymnasmata (see Theon, *Prog.* 10).[58] Likewise, the student of the progymnasmata learned to write chreiai of various types (see *Prog.* 210.3-6).[59] These chreia were vignettes which celebrated the words and deeds of famous men, and Luke shows himself adept at their composition. One cannot but agree with Vernon Robbins's assessment of Luke: 'The primary culture exhibited by his social location is written literature and cultivated speech'.[60]

54. Arthur A. Just, Jr, *Luke* (Concordia Commentary; St Louis: Concordia Publishing House, 1996), 37.

55. Erhardt Güttgemans, 'In welchem Sinne ist Lukas "Historiker"? Die Beziehungen von Luk 1, 1-4 und Papias zur antiken Rhetorik', *LingBib* 54 (1983), 9-26.

56. See Theon, *Prog.* 8.

57. See Marion Soards, *The Speeches in Acts: Their Content, Context, and Concerns* (Louisville, KY: Westminster/John Knox Press, 1994). Kennedy, *New Testament Interpretation*, 114-40. See also Jerome Neyrey, 'The Forensic Defense Speech in Acts 22–26: Form and Function', in Charles H. Talbert (ed.), *Luke–Acts: New Perspectives from the Society of Biblical Literature Seminar* (New York: Crossroad, 1984), 210-24.

58. For a discussion of Luke's use of speeches, see Aune, *The New Testament*, 124-28.

59. See Burton Mack and Vernon Robbins, 'Elaboration of the Chreia in the Hellenistic School', in *iidem* (eds.), *Patterns of Persuasion in the Gospel* (Sonoma, CA: Polebridge Press, 1989), 31-67.

60. Robbins, 'The Social Location of the Implied Author', 332.

b. *Evidence of Luke's Rhetorical Praise of Jesus*

Luke's Gospel has been classified as biography, history, apologetic historiography, and simply as a 'gospel'.[61] Philip Shuler has argued persuasively that the Gospels exhibit many of the characteristics of encomiastic biography.[62] Others have rightly cautioned against classifying Luke according to the genre of biography, noting its peculiar traits, as well as its relationship to the book of Acts. However, as is the case with Plutarch's *Lives*, we recognize that encomiastic elements permeate the Gospel of Luke. As we consider how Luke made use of encomiastic techniques throughout his work, we should not be surprised that Luke depicted Jesus' death in encomiastic terms as well.

As a Hellenistic writer trained in rhetoric, Luke learned the rhetorical conventions for praise and blame, and employed them in the writing of his Gospel. According to Theon, an encomium includes the following elements: (1) origin and birth, (2) nurture and training, (3) accomplishments and deeds, and (4) comparison. Luke makes use of these elements in praise of Jesus, and thereby demonstrates his own rhetorical training and familiarity with the values embedded within the rhetoric.

c. *Luke's Encomiastic Treatment of Jesus*

(1) *Origin and birth.* The rhetorical sources we have studied tell us that a person's race, country, ancestors, and parents are proper subjects for praise. According to the rhetoricians, noble lands, cities, and families produce noble children. Theon labels such factors 'good breeding' (εὐγενίας) (*Prog.* 9.58). Therefore, Aristotle writes, 'Again, all such actions as are in accord with what is fitting are noble; if,

61. Karl Ludwig Schmidt's thesis that the Gospels were *sui generis* was long considered definitive. See Schmidt's 'Die Stellung der Evangelien in der allgemeinen Literaturgeschichte', in Hans Schmidt (ed.), *Eucharisterion: Studien zur Religion und Literatur des Alten und Neuen Testaments; Hermann Gunkel zum 60 Geburtstag* (Göttingen: Vandenhoeck & Ruprecht, 1923), 50-134. Charles Talbert, among others, classifies the Gospels as *Vitae.* See Talbert, *What is a Gospel?* (Philadelphia: Fortress Press, 1977). Others classify Luke–Acts as a history of the Christian religion. Gregory Sterling (*Historiography and Self-Definition*) defines Luke–Acts more specifically as apologetic historiography.

62. Shuler argued that Matthew is an 'encomium biography' in *A Genre for the Gospels.* He presents similar arguments concerning Luke in 'The Genre(s) of the Gospels', in D.L. Dugan (ed.), *The Interrelations of the Gospels* (Leuven: Leuven University Press, 1984), 459-83. For further discussion on the Gospels as biography, see Richard Burridge, *What are the Gospels? A Comparison with Graeco-Roman Biography* (Cambridge: Cambridge University Press, 1992).

for instance, they are worthy of a man's ancestors' (*Rhet.* 1.9.31). Accordingly, funeral orators typically claimed that the fallen were worthy of their ancestry. For instance, Hyperides tells us that the Athenians 'born of their own country' share 'a lineage of unrivaled purity' (*F.S.* 7).

Portents, signs, and visions also may accompany birth and be a cause for praise. For instance, when Cicero was born, Plutarch reports, 'a phantom appeared to his nurse and foretold that her charge would be a great blessing to all the Romans' (*Cic.* 2.1).

Luke has much to say about Jesus' praiseworthy origins. His mother Mary was cousin to Elizabeth, 'one of the daughters of Aaron', whose husband was a 'priest of the division of Abijah' (Lk. 1.5). As such, Jesus was honorably related to priestly stock. Joseph likewise had an honorable lineage, being from 'the house of David' (1.27; 2.4). Hence Jesus belonged to priestly and royal stock, the two most noble tribes in Judea. Mary, further, is depicted as a humble, pious woman, the 'Lord's servant' (1.38). Such humility was a highly valued feminine virtue.[63] Furthermore, an angel announces his birth (1.27), and two prophets sing his praise (2.29-32, 38). The genealogy (3.23-38) links Jesus to the honorable and illustrious history of Israel, culminating in the claim that his ultimate paternity is from Adam and finally God.[64] Interestingly, in the 'Parable of the Ten Talents' Jesus compares himself to a man 'of noble birth' (εὐγενής) who went to a far country in order to be made king (19.12). Evidently, Jesus was claiming his ascribed royal status as the son of David and son of God (see 1.32). This claim for royalty would have also been understood as a rhetorical claim for honor.

(2) *Phenomena at birth.* As we have seen, the rhetor is trained to note any unusual or supernatural phenomena which may have occurred at birth, which give evidence that a person has been in some way marked out by the gods. In Luke, the signs include the appearance of the angels (Lk. 1.26; 2.8-14) and an extraordinary virgin birth (1.34). Gabriel, the messenger from God, tells Mary that she will give birth 'to the son of the most high God', and that 'the Lord God will give him the throne of his father, David' (1.32).

63. For a discussion of the feminine virtues, see Malina, *The New Testament World*, esp. 50-53.

64. Fitzmyer, with others, recognizes a connection between Jesus' sonship at baptism and the genealogical claim that he is the 'son of God' (Fitzmyer, *Luke*, I, 491).

(3) *Nurture and training*. The encomia inform us that a person's nurture and training are subjects fit for praise. Aphthonius instructs would-be writers: '[T]hen you will take up education, which you will divide into inclination to study, talent, and rules'.[65]

The ancients understood that the virtues and successes of adulthood could be seen already in childhood. Accordingly, Plutarch notes that Cicero's literary and rhetorical talents were evident even in childhood:

> [H]is natural talent shone out clear and he won name and fame among the boys, so that their fathers used to visit the schools in order to see Cicero with their own eyes and observe the quickness and intelligence in his studies for which he was extolled. (*Cic.* 2.2)[66]

Of the Gospel writers, Luke alone tells of Jesus' boyhood and training. In particular, Luke reports Jesus' boyhood teaching at the temple where he 'astonished' the teachers with his answers to their questions (Lk. 2.46). Jesus, the ultimate *Wunderkind*, surpasses the honor due a prodigious student; he teaches the teachers. Of this incident, Danker comments, 'Luke's incorporation of such type of encomium or eulogy therefore advances his thematic stress on Jesus as an Israelite of exceptional merit'.[67] Indeed, Jesus' boyhood wisdom is a sign that his excellence is truly innate, not accrued by chance or circumstance.

Luke punctuates Jesus' boyhood development by telling the reader/hearer that 'Jesus increased in wisdom (σοφίᾳ) and stature (ἡλικίᾳ), and in favor (χάριτι) with God and man' (2.52). Though Luke's description echoes the Old Testament account of Samuel's development (1 Sam. 2.21, 26),[68] it is also a Greco-Roman rhetorical device which demonstrates that Jesus' exceptional excellence is long standing. As Danker writes, 'The Hellenistic cast of the verse would signify to a Greco-Roman public that Jesus is to be understood as a person of exceptional merit, deserving of public recognition'.[69]

65. Nadeau, 'The Progymnasmata of Aphthonius', 273.

66. Plutarch also tells us that Alexander, as a boy, showed the type of self-restraint which would later make him great (*Alex.* 4.4). Josephus likewise speaks of himself as precocious (*Life* 8–12). Rudolf Bultmann lists similar stories of child prodigies, to be found in the writings of Philo, Herodotus, and Philostratus, among others, in his *History of the Synoptic Tradition* (trans. John Marsh; New York: Harper & Row, 1976), 300-301.

67. Danker, *Jesus and the New Age*, 76.

68. See Fitzmyer, *Luke*, II, 446.

69. Danker, *Jesus and the New Age*, 79.

(4) *Accomplishments and deeds.* The rhetorician was trained to praise his subjects for deeds of body and soul. According to Theon, deeds of the body include such attributes as health, strength, beauty, and quick sensibility (*Prog.* 9.20). Luke tells us nothing about Jesus' physical appearance, and little about his physical prowess, though we do know that he evidenced physical endurance during the forty-day fast (Lk. 4.1-13), a difficult ministry (9.58), and the beating (22.63), flogging (23.16), and crucifixion (23.33-36). Luke offers more of what rhetoricians designate as deeds of the soul, namely, virtues such as justice, wisdom, temperance, courage, and piety (see Theon, *Prog.* 9.22-24; Menander Rhetor, *Treatise* 2.373.5-14; Quintilian, *Inst. Orat.* 3.7.15; Aristotle, *Rhet.* 1.9.5-13).

(5) *Deeds of justice/righteousness.* As we have seen, Pseudo-Aristotle defines righteousness (δικαιοσύνη) as the fulfilling of one's duties toward God, country, and parents (*Virt. vit.* 5.2-3, 16-24). This definition is further amplified by Menander Rhetor: 'The parts of justice are piety, fair dealing, and reverence: piety towards the gods, fair dealing towards men, reverence towards the departed' (*Treatise* 1.17-20). Elsewhere, he adds, 'Under justice, you should include humanity to subjects, gentleness of character and approachability, integrity and incorruptibility in matters of justice, freedom from partiality and from prejudice in giving judicial decisions, equal treatment of rich and poor' (*Treatise* 2.5-10).

The ancients understood righteousness to include piety towards the gods. According to Menander Rhetor, piety (εὐσέβεια) consists of two elements: being god-loved (θεοφιλότης) and god-loving (φιλοθεότης).

> The former means being loved by the gods and receiving many blessings from them, the latter consists of loving the gods and having a relationship of friendship with them. (*Treatise* 1.361.20-25)

Throughout his work, Luke depicts Jesus as being both God-loved and God-loving, as we would expect according to rhetorical convention. The child Jesus owes his birth to the Holy Spirit and 'God's power' (Lk. 1.35). We are told that the boy Jesus grew in 'favor (χάριτι) with God' (2.52). At Jesus' baptism, God calls Jesus 'beloved' (ἀγαπητός) (3.21-22). In all of this, Jesus is shown to be 'God-loved'. He is also 'God-loving'. At his temptation, Jesus pledges his obedience to God (4.1-13). Furthermore, we are told that Jesus, in fulfillment of his duties towards God, journeyed annually to Jerusalem for the Passover (2.41-42), and attended synagogue on the Sabbath 'according to his custom' (4.16). Luke further highlights Jesus' righteousness towards God by depicting him as a man of prayer (3.21; 6.12; 9.18, 28; 11.2; 22.32, 41; 23.46). These examples point to Jesus as 'God-loving', and therefore pious and righteous.

Part of righteousness includes fulfilling one's duty towards one's country. Accordingly, Jesus urges the people to fulfill their duties towards the government: 'Give to Caesar what belongs to Caesar' (20.25). Again, Jesus is called the 'glory' of his people Israel (2.32).

A third part of righteousness is the fulfillment of one's duty towards parents. While teaching that discipleship takes precedence over family obligations (see 9.59-61; 12.52-53; 14.26), Jesus himself fulfilled his earthly obligations to his parents. Thus, Luke tells us that the boy Jesus was 'obedient' (ἦν ὑποτασσόμενος) to his parents (2.51).

As Menander Rhetor notes, the just man has a gentle character, who is approachable by all people, showing no partiality towards the rich. We see Jesus' gentle character in the raising of the widow's son, where we are told 'his heart went out to her' (Lk. 7.13), and in his lament for Jerusalem, where he compares himself to a mother hen (13.34). We see his approachability in the way he allows the sinful woman to anoint his feet, and then stands up to the powerful Pharisees who challenge her presence (7.36-50). We see it again in the way that Jesus allows the little children to approach him (18.15-17). Repeatedly, people come to Jesus who readily hears and grants their requests (see, e.g., Lk. 8.49-50; 9.38; 17.11-19; 18.35). Time and again, we see that Jesus shows no partiality towards the rich and powerful. He accepts the wealthy Zacchaeus (19.1-9), but not because of his money. On the contrary, he speaks bold truth to the wealthy (i.e. Lk. 12.13-21; 16.19-31; 18.18-29). In all of these actions, the student of rhetoric would have seen a man who performed great deeds of justice.

(6) *Deeds of wisdom*. Aristotle defines wisdom (φρόνησις) as 'a virtue of reason, which enables men to come to a wise decision in regard to good and evil things' (*Rhet.* 1.9.8). Elsewhere, he offers a fuller definition:

> It belongs to wisdom (φρόνησις) to take counsel, to judge the goods and evils and all the things in life that are desirable and to be avoided, to use all the available goods finely, to behave rightly in society, to observe due occasions, to employ both speech and action with sagacity, to have expert knowledge of all things that are useful. Memory and experience and acuteness are each of them either a consequence or a concomitant of wisdom. (*Virt. vit.* 4.1-2)

Wisdom (φρόνησις), for Aristotle, is an eminently practical virtue that enables a person to perceive his situation rightly, and to speak and act in an appropriate and beneficial manner.[70] Luke never explicitly labels Jesus as possessing φρόνησις, however, though he does paint a picture of a man who knows how to negotiate the practical difficulties and obstacles of life.

For one, Jesus displays wisdom in the way he speaks. His words cause the people to marvel (Lk. 4.22). At a number of symposia Jesus is depicted as a wise man who is able to discern the situation and respond with a poignant story (see 5.27-39; 7.36-50; 14.1-24). Jesus' wisdom as a speaker is seen especially in the controversy stories. When Jesus is challenged about fasting (5.33-39), working on the Sabbath (6.1-5), and healing on the Sabbath (6.6-11), Jesus responds in such a way as to silence and humiliate his critics.

Often, Luke will depict Jesus' wisdom by the recounting of chreia. Students commonly studied chreia as part of the preliminary exercises of rhetoric.[71] Chreia, Aelius Theon tells us, are 'concise statements or actions...attributed to a definite character', and which may become the basis for an expanded narrative argument.[72] As Hock and O'Neil remind us, 'Chreiai celebrate a philosopher's wit, or at least his quick-wittedness'.[73] By the recording of chreia, Luke depicts Jesus as a man with practical wisdom, who knows how to coin a phrase in order to make mute his critics. Well-recognized chreia include Jesus' words to the Pharisees and scribes: 'It is not the healthy who need a doctor, but the sick' (Lk. 5.31); 'My mother and brothers are those who hear God's word and put it into practice' (8.21); 'Where there is a dead body, there the vultures will gather' (17.37).

Jesus' verbal prowess is especially evident as he approaches the cross. Concerning the frustration of Jesus' opponents, Luke writes, 'They were unable to trap him in what he had said there in public. And astonished by his answer, they became silent' (Lk. 20.26). When responding to challenging questions concerning the resurrection and marriage, Jesus again silences his critics, so that 'No one dared to ask him any more questions' (20.39).

70. See Ulrich Wilckens, 'σοφία', in *TDNT*, VII, 465-96.

71. See Ronald F. Hock and Edward N. O'Neil, *The Chreia in Ancient Rhetoric. I. The Progymnasmata* (SBLTT, 27; Greco-Roman Religion, 9; Atlanta: Scholars Press, 1986), 3-47; Bonner, *Education in Ancient Rome*, 176, 253.

72. Aelius Theon, 'On Chreia', 2-4, in Hock and O'Neil, *The Chreia*, 82.

73. Hock and O'Neil, *The Chreia*, 5.

Pseudo-Aristotle describes a wise man as one who is able 'to judge the goods from the evils' (*Virt. vit.* 4.1). So also, Jesus resists the temptations of Satan (Lk. 4.1-13). Again, Aristotle describes the wise man as one who discerns between things which are 'desirable and to be avoided' (*Virt. vit.* 4.1). Accordingly, the Lukan Jesus 'walked right through the crowd at Nazareth', because he knew that the time of his passion was not at hand (Lk. 4.30). As, however, the right time approached, 'Jesus resolutely set out for Jerusalem' (9.51). As a man of wisdom, he understood that he would have to undergo the passion and then rise again (18.31).

(7) *Deeds of temperance/self-control.* Aristotle defines temperance (σοφροσύνη) as that quality which 'disposes men in regard to the pleasures of the body as the law prescribes; the contrary is licentiousness' (*Rhet.* 1.9.8). Luke demonstrates Jesus' σωφροσύνη by recounting the temptations in the desert, especially the temptation to turn stones into bread.[74]

(8) *Deeds of manliness/courage.* Aristotle defines courage (ἀνδρεία) as 'the virtue that disposes men to do noble deeds in situations of danger, in accordance with the law and in obedience to its commands' (*Rhet.* 1.9.8). For Aristotle, the courageous man, therefore, 'fearlessly confronts a noble death' (*Eth. nic.* 3.6.10). Luke demonstrates Jesus' courage in his resolute determination to go to Jerusalem (9.51). Jesus' determination never wanes, though he knows he will be flogged and ultimately put to death (18.32). All the while, Jesus preaches boldly and openly, both concomitant to the virtue of courage.

(9) *Jesus' magnanimity.* In the study of epideictic rhetoric, students were taught to praise the philanthropy (φιλανθρωπία) and magnanimity (μεγαλοψυχία) of their subjects. Philanthropy is 'productive of great benefits', while the closely aligned virtue of magnanimity 'does good in many matters' (Aristotle, *Rhet.* 1.9.8). Accordingly, Theon instructs his students: 'Noble actions are also those which we do for the sake of others' (*Prog.* 9.31).

Luke, as cultural bridge-builder, depicts Jesus as a magnanimous and philanthropic benefactor, who 'went about doing good (διῆλθεν εὐεργετῶν)' (Acts 10.38). Jesus displays his beneficence in acting as a savior (Lk. 2.11; Acts 5.31; 13.23), who provides salvation (Lk. 6.9;

74. For a discussion of this as an example of self-control, see Neyrey, *Honor and Shame in the Gospel of Matthew*, 121.

7.50; 8.36, 48, 50; 9.56; 17.19; 18.42; 19.9,10; Acts 2.1, 40, 47; 4.9, 12: 11.14; 14.9; 15.11; 16.31). For Luke, Jesus is a physician, whose salvation is comprehensive, and brings wholeness to body and soul (see Lk. 4.23; 5.31).[75] This healing also brought sinners to repentance, and rid people of evil spirits (see Lk. 5.27-32; 8.26-39). Compared to Matthew//Mark, Luke's accounts of Jesus' healing often emphasize the great number of beneficiaries (see Lk. 4.40-41; 6.19; 9.16). Luke furthermore provides stories of healing not found in Matthew// Mark (see Lk. 7.12-17; 13.10-17; 14.1-6; 17.12-19). In the ancient world, healing was considered an act of magnanimity and beneficence, worthy of public honor.[76] As such, the effect of the healing stories is to demonstrate Jesus' widespread magnanimity, which is offered to all segments of society, including men, women, and children, as well as the marginalized, such as the unclean lepers (5.12-13; 17.11-19). We further see Jesus' magnanimity on display in his feeding miracle, in which his multiplication of the loaves benefits a large crowd (9.10-17).

(10) *Luke's use of comparison/synkrisis.* The use of comparison/synkrisis was a means by which a rhetor amplified the praise of his subject. Aristotle encourages the encomiast to compare his subject with other famous people:

> And you must compare him with illustrious personages, for it affords ground for amplification and is noble, if he can be proved better than men of worth. Amplification is with good reason ranked as one of the forms of praise, since it consists in superiority, and superiority is one of the things that are noble. (*Rhet.* 1.39)

The grounds for comparing individuals include nobility of birth, education, and reputation, as well as the other qualities and virtues listed in the prescriptions for writing encomia (see Theon, *Prog.* 10.27-34). The use of synkrisis, as we have seen, lies at the heart of Plutarch's *Lives.* According to Menander Rhetor, comparisons should be made between like things:

> You must not forget our previous proposition, namely that comparisons should be made under each head; these comparisons, however, will be partial (e.g. education with education, temperance with temperance), whereas the complete one will concern the whole subject, as when we compare a reign as a whole and in sum with another reign, e.g., the reign of Alexander with the present one. (*Treatise* 2.377.1-9)

75. For a discussion of healing as wholesomeness, see John J. Pilch, 'Sickness and Healing in Luke-Acts', in Neyrey (ed.), *The Social World of Luke-Acts*, 181-209.

76. For a discussion of healing as beneficence, see Danker, *Jesus and the New Age*, esp. 7-8.

This is exactly what Luke does in his detailed comparison of Jesus and John the Baptist regarding the respective accounts of their birth, growth, and ministry.

Drawing upon his rhetorical training, Luke includes an extensive synkrisis in his step-parallelism of Jesus and John the Baptist in his infancy narrative: (1) the parents are introduced (Lk. 1.5-7//1.26-27); (2) birth announcement and appearance of an angel (1.18-23//1.28-38); (3) conception (1.23-25//2.5); (d) birth and naming (1.59-66//2.6-7, 21); (5) response 1.67-79//2.22-38); (6) growth of child (1.80//2.39-40, 52). This parallelism, Raymond Brown notes, continues in the depiction of John and Jesus' ministry:

> JBap and Jesus both in the desert (3.2; 4.1).
>
> JBap and Jesus both written of by Isaiah (3.4-6; 4.17-19).
>
> JBap and Jesus both issued warnings drawn from Old Testament (3.7-9; 4.24-27).
>
> JBap and Jesus both questioned about identity (3.15; 4.34).
>
> JBap and Jesus both preached the good news (3.18; 4.43).[77]

Repeatedly, John's prominence is highlighted so that Jesus' superiority can be demonstrated.

John himself acknowledges that he is 'not worthy to untie the strap of [Jesus'] sandals' (Lk. 3.16). The rhetorical effect is to demonstrate the praiseworthy status of Jesus.

8. *Summary*

In the Greco-Roman world, rhetoric was a powerful tool for transmitting the values of the culture. The values embedded within the rhetoric of Aristotle remained largely constant, even until the time when Luke–Acts was written. Epideictic rhetoric, in particular, offered specific rules for offering praise. We see in the Athenian funeral speeches and in Plutarch's *Lives* that the rhetor was trained to praise certain features of a person's life. Many of these same features were applicable when praising a person's death. This tradition of a praiseworthy death was long-standing and consistent. The tradition of the noble death was explicit and detailed.

Furthermore, we have seen how the progymnasmata, the educational rhetoric of the day, distilled the values of epideictic rhetoric

77. Raymond Brown, *The Birth of the Messiah: A Commentary on the Gospels of Matthew and Luke* (ABRL; Garden City, NY: Doubleday, rev. edn, 1993), 250.

to those who were literate in the ancient world. Moreover, we are persuaded that literacy and rhetoric were largely coterminous.

Finally, we have seen that Luke–Acts itself displays much evidence that Luke was a rhetorically trained writer. Not only does Luke display his training through the writing of historical prefaces and speeches, but he specifically makes use of epideictic rhetoric in his praise of Jesus. All of this evidence leads us to think that it is highly probable that the values embedded in epideictic literature affected the way in which Luke depicted Jesus' life. There is much evidence to suggest Luke made use of the rhetoric of praise in the writing of his passion account.

3

THE DEATH OF SOCRATES AND THE LUKAN PASSION

1. *Introduction*

In exploring possible tools and sources which Luke used in constructing his passion narrative, we move from the general field of epideictic rhetoric to the specific possibility that Luke drew directly upon the story of Socrates' death to shape his account.

The original Greco-Roman concept of the noble death had its roots in the martial virtues of courage and duty in battle. We see this martial nobility in Sophocles' account of Homer's warrior-hero Ajax, who chose honorable death over shameful life: 'Let a man live nobly or die nobly' (*Ajax* 480). With the death of Socrates, we have something new: a wise man who dies righteously and virtuously for the sake of his philosophy and the truth. A.W.H. Adkins has argued that the latter part of the fifth-century marked the time when the competitive, martial virtues were replaced by 'co-operative excellences' to meet the 'democratic aspirations' of the emerging city-state.[1] With Socrates, we have a new type of hero, one who stands on the battlefield of ideas. As Herbert Musurillo writes, 'The death of Socrates, especially as idealized by Plato, was a powerful influence in the development of the idea of death as a heroic ideal'.[2]

The ancients esteemed Socrates' death as most noble and praiseworthy, and his story was familiar to the educated of Luke's day. Moreover, there is evidence that Luke was sensitive to the fact that the Matthean and Markan pictures of Jesus' death did not match well with Greco-Roman ideals of a noble death as epitomized by Socrates. Raymond Brown writes:

1. A.W.H. Adkins, *Moral Values and Political Behaviour in Ancient Greece: From Homer to the End of the Fifth Century* (New York: W.W. Norton, 1972), esp. 112-19; see also his *Merit and Responsibility*.
2. Musurillo, *The Acts of the Pagan Martyrs*, 237.

> Educated Greco-Roman pagans would have been familiar with the death of Socrates described by Plato. Execution by self-administered poison was forced upon this philosopher of lofty principles who was innocent of crime. Without tears and without impassioned pleas to be spared, he accepted his fate, nobly encouraging his followers not to grieve... Consequently, hearers/readers imbued with Platonic/Socratic ideals might react disparagingly toward the Mark/Matt picture of a Jesus distraught and troubled, throwing himself prostrate to the ground and begging God to deliver him.[3]

Therefore, we may well ask whether Luke consciously drew from the story of Socrates to shape his own passion narrative.

2. *Status Quaestionis*

The possible influence of the Socrates story on the Lukan passion narrative is a question rarely touched upon, even by those who are wont to take note of Greco-Roman influence on Luke–Acts.

Often, if Socrates is mentioned, it is for the purpose of contrasting the equanimity of the philosopher with the agony of Jesus. Frederick Danker notes that in the Mount of Olives scene, 'Luke does not recreate Plato's *Phaedo* in which Sokrates is portrayed as one who accepts death heroically'.[4] Likewise, Oscar Cullman contrasts the calm equanimity with which Socrates drank hemlock with the dread which afflicted Jesus.[5] We will contend, however, that Luke draws comparisons to the two great figures.

The possibility that Luke made use of the Socrates story has been broached in an exploratory article by John Kloppenborg. He notes three motifs common to both Plato's and Luke's accounts: (1) both the *Phaedo* and the Lukan passion employ the literary form of a 'Last Discourse'/'Farewell Symposium'; (2) both pay attention to the '*Ars Moriendi*', that is, 'the way the hero dies'; (3) both emphasize the role of friends.[6] These comparisons, among others, are worth exploring. More recently, Gregory Sterling has argued that Luke does indeed make use of the Socrates story, and that it 'sounds gently' in the passion narrative.[7] In particular, Sterling points to the courage with

3. Brown, *The Death of the Messiah*, I, 217.
4. Danker, *Jesus and the New Age*, 354.
5. Oscar Cullman, 'Immortality of the Soul or Resurrection of the Dead: The Witness of the New Testament', in Krister Stendahl (ed.), *Immortality and Resurrection* (New York: Macmillan, 1965), 12-20.
6. Kloppenborg, '"Exitus clari viri"'.
7. Sterling, 'Mors philosophi', 2.

which Jesus faced death, and the fact that he died according to divine necessity. These are points of similarity that I also will note.

3. *The Influence of Plato's* Phaedo, Euthyphro, Apology, *and* Crito *in the Hellenistic World*

a. *The Widespread Influence of the Socrates Story*

Before continuing with a comparison of the Lukan passion and the Socrates story, we do well to note the latter's popularity among the ancients. The story of Socrates' death was not merely the relic of an obscure past, but part of the collective memory of Greco-Roman civilization. The Socrates story finds its way into Hellenistic-Jewish literature as well.

Plato's *Phaedo* contains the critical text of Socrates' death, while *Euthyphro*, *Apology*, and *Crito* provide the important context for understanding Socrates' attitude towards death, as well as the circumstances which attended it. Scholars note that the *Phaedo* achieved a type of 'canonical status' in the ancient world.[8] The story of Socrates' death served as a paradigm of the just man who faces unjust death with courage and serenity.[9] As Lucian of Samosota (120–180 CE) put it, Socrates is 'praised everywhere' (*Somnium* 13). Klaus Döring has demonstrated the widespread influence which the story of Socrates' death had on such popular philosophers as Seneca, Cicero, Epictetus, and Plutarch.[10] In their work on voluntary death in the ancient world, Droge and Tabor echo Döring's sentiment, noting that the importance of the *Phaedo* 'can hardly be exaggerated'.[11]

b. *Socrates and the Popular Philosophers*

Among popular philosophers such as Cicero, Seneca, and Epictetus, the well-known death of Socrates was employed as an example for others to follow. Cicero (106–43 BCE) lauded the death of Cato Uticensis by comparing it to that of Socrates. God had given Cato permission to die, 'as he did in the past to Socrates' (*Tusc*. 1.71-74).

8. See Leendert G. Westerink, *The Greek Commentaries on Plato's Phaedo* (Amsterdam: North-Holland), 7.

9. See Werner Jaeger's *Paideia: The Ideals of Greek Culture* (3 vols.; New York: Oxford University Press, 1943), II, 13.

10. Klaus Döring, *Exemplum Socratis: Studien zur Sokratesnachwirkung in der kynisch-stoischen Popularphilosophie der frühen Kaiserzeit und im frühen Christentum* (Hermes Einzelschriften, 42: Wiesbaden: Franz Steiner, 1979), 39.

11. Droge and Tabor, *A Noble Death*, 22.

Likewise, Seneca (4 BCE–65 CE), writing in the same century as Luke, praises the death of Cato by coloring it with images from the Socrates story:

> But why should I not tell you about Cato, how he read Plato's book on that last glorious night, with a sword laid at his pillow. He had provided these two requisites for his last moment—the first that he might have the will to die, and second, that he might have the means. (*Ep*. 24.6-7)

Seneca could be sure that his reader understood the significance of 'Plato's book', which depicted the death of Socrates and provided a noble example of how to die. Elsewhere in the same epistle, Seneca praised Socrates as one who willingly faced death 'in order to free mankind from the fear of two most grievous things, death and imprisonment' (*Ep*. 24.4).

Epictetus often held up Socrates' fearlessness of death for emulation and inspiration. The memory of Socrates was especially useful as a paradigm for how to die well:

> If it were useful to men by living, should we not have done much more good to men by dying when we ought, and as we ought? And now that Socrates is dead the memory of him is no less useful to men, nay, is perhaps even more useful, than what he did or said while he lived. (*Ench*. 4.1.68-69)[12]

Similarly, the death of Socrates finds its way into the *Lives* of Plutarch. For Plutarch, Socrates was a prime example of misunderstood greatness, who 'lost his life for the sake of philosophy' (*Nic*. 23.3). Plutarch further tells us that Cato, in emulation of Socrates, read the *Phaedo* before taking his life (*Cat. Min*. 67–68). Elsewhere Plutarch reports that the Athenians repented of treating Phocion as poorly and unjustly as they had once treated Socrates (*Phoc*. 38.5). Again, throughout Plutarch's *Moralia*, Socrates' death is held up for emulation. Plutarch holds up Socrates' example of calm and cheerfulness (*An vit*. 499B); his teaching while in prison (*Tranq. an*. 466E-F); his virtue under duress (*Virt. prof*. 84F); and his fearlessness (*Cons. Apoll*. 108E). In fact, Plutarch bases an entire dialogue on the interpretation of the divine sign given to Socrates at his death (*Gen. Socr*.). The works of Plutarch, especially the latter, assume that his readers would have known the story of Socrates and his death.

12. See also *Ench*. 1.2.33; 1.2.36; 1.4.24, etc. For a further discussion on influence of Socrates on Epictetus, see Döring's *Exemplum Socratis*, 52-54.

Socrates' enduring legacy can be seen in the third-century biographer, Diogenes Laertius, who dedicates a chapter to him in his *Lives and Opinions of Eminent Philosophers*.[13]

c. *Socrates and the Educational System*

Indeed, the death of Socrates and other famous men appears to have been fodder not only for the philosophers, but standard fare in Greco-Roman education. We see this in the exasperation of Seneca, who, having mentioned the death of Socrates and others, writes, '"Oh", you say, "those stories have been droned to death in all the schools"' (*Ep*. 24.6).

The story of Socrates' death found its way into the primary rhetorical handbooks and is referred to in one of the chreia in the progymnasmata of Theon:

> Socrates the philosopher, when a certain student named Apollodorus said to him, 'The Athenians have unjustly condemned you to death', said with a laugh, 'But did you want them to do it justly?'[14]

This same saying was cited by Xenophon (*Apol*. 28; *Mem*. 4.8.9), Seneca (*Constan*. 7.3), and Diogenes Laertius (*Socr*. 2.35).

d. *Socrates in the Greco-Roman World: A Summary*

From the time of Socrates well into the Roman Empire, the ancients seem to have concurred with Xenophon's verdict: 'In fact it is admitted that there is no record of death more nobly borne' (*Mem*. 4.7.2).[15] Werner Jaeger sums up nicely the place of Socrates in the ancient mind:

> Socrates is one of the imperishable figures who have become symbolic. The real man...shed most of his personality as he entered history and become for all eternity a 'representative man'. It was not really his life or his doctrine (so far as he had any doctrine) which raised him to such eminence, so much as the death he suffered for the conviction on which his life was founded.[16]

13. For a discussion of Diogenes Laertius's work, see Luis E. Navia, *Socratic Testimonies* (Lanham, MD: University Press of America, 1987), 321-25.
14. See Hock and O'Neil, *The Chreia*, 90-91. This story of Socrates also appears in Diogenes Laertius's *Socr*. 2.35.
15. Xenophon, in a rhetorical flourish, asks, 'How then, could man die more nobly? Or what death could be nobler than the death most nobly faced?' (*Mem*. 4.8.3).
16. Jaeger, *Paideia*, II, 13.

e. *The Story of Socrates in the Maccabean Literature*

Socrates' influence was not limited to Greeks and Romans. The Hellenistic–Jewish martyrological accounts of 2 and 4 *Maccabees* likewise bear the influence of the figure of Socrates. This is significant, for it demonstrates that knowledge of the Socrates story was not limited to the Greeks and Romans, but found its way into Hellenistic–Jewish literature of Luke's day.

As Moses Hadas says of the main character, 'Eleazar is like Socrates at too many points for the resemblance to be accidental'.[17] In particular, Hadas compares Eleazar's 'gallant impatience' to die with that of Socrates.[18] J.A. Goldstein and Moses Hadas point to Eleazar's words upon death: 'To young men I shall have left a noble example of how to die happily and nobly in behalf of our revered and holy laws' (2 Macc. 6.28). Both commentators find these words highly reminiscent of Socrates.[19] Goldstein identifies no less than seven points of resemblance between Socrates and Eleazar: (1) their old age; (2) fear of death cannot make them yield; (3) this attitude is the culmination of a lifetime of virtue; (4) they reject an easier alternative; (5) they refuse to transgress the law; (6) they assume the inevitability of divine punishment; (7) their opponents are offended by the speeches which they make. All of which leads Goldstein to comment, 'No educated Greek could miss the resemblance of Eleazar to Socrates'.[20] Such similarities between Socrates and Eleazar have led Jan Willem van Henten to portray the Maccabean martyrs as Jewish philosophers in the mold of Socrates.[21]

f. *The Story of Socrates in Josephus*

Likewise, Josephus demonstrates acquaintance with the Socrates story. Josephus, a contemporary of Luke, was born into a priestly family and grew up in Jerusalem (see *Life* 1–2). His later ties with the

17. Moses Hadas, *The Third and Fourth Books of Maccabees: Jewish Apocryphal Literature* (ed. and trans. Moses Hadas; New York: Ktav, 1953), 101.

18. As the guard offers Socrates the poison, he tells him, 'Do not hurry', but Socrates tells the guard that he will 'gain nothing by taking the poison later', and asks that the guard continue with the execution: 'Do as I ask and do not refuse' (*Phaedo* 117A). Similarly, Eleazar tells his executioner, 'Do not delay' (*4 Macc.* 6.23). See Hadas, *Maccabees*, 180.

19. Hadas, *Maccabees*, 117; J.A. Goldstein, *II Maccabees* (AB, 41A; Garden City, NY: Doubleday, 1983), 285.

20. Goldstein, *II Maccabees*, 285.

21. See Jan Willem van Henten, *The Maccabean Martyrs as Saviours of the Jewish People: A Study of 2 and 4 Maccabees* (Leiden: E.J. Brill, 1997), esp. 270-78.

Roman emperor Vespasian, whom he prophesied would become the next Roman emperor, are as well known as they are controversial.[22] Like Luke, Josephus was a man thoroughly at home in both the Jewish and Hellenistic worlds.

In his apologetic work *Against Apion*, Josephus strikes against the anti-Semitic prejudices of his day and defends his own religion over and against ideas current among the Greeks. Among the stories which Josephus cites in his apology is Socrates' death. In particular, he reminds his audience that the Athenians, famous for openness, failed greatly when it came to treating their most illustrious citizen:

> But the Athenians, who considered their city open to all comers—what was their attitude in this matter? Apollonius was ignorant of this, and of the inexorable penalty which they inflicted on any who uttered a single word about the gods contrary to their laws. On what other grounds was Socrates put to death? He never sought to betray his city to the enemy, he robbed no temple. No; because he used to swear strange oaths and give out (in jest, surely, as some say) that he received communications from a spirit, he was therefore condemned to die by drinking hemlock. His accuser brought a further charge against him of corrupting young men, because he stimulated them to hold the constitution and laws of their country in contempt. Such was the punishment of Socrates, a citizen of Athens. (*Apion* 2.262-66)

What are we to conclude from Josephus's description of Socrates death? First, we can say that Josephus was very familiar with the story, able to draw on a number of its details, namely: (1) the charges against Socrates, (2) that he swore strange oaths, (3) that he is said to have communications from a spirit, (4) that poison hemlock was the method of execution. Secondly, the story of Socrates was a current topic of conversation, as evidenced by the debate over whether Socrates was jesting concerning the spirits (*Apion* 2.263). Thirdly, we may assume that the reader would have known the story well enough to follow Josephus' argument. This is significant, for it is further evidence that Socrates' story was known among a wide audience of people, including Hellenized Jews.

g. *Socrates and Peregrinus: The 'Christian Socrates'*

Evidently, from an early period, some Christians also drew comparisons between Christ and Socrates. Lucian of Samosota (c. 120–200 CE) satirizes such claims in a sketch of the charlatan Peregrinus, a converted Christian, who soon became a leader. For his teaching activity

22. See H. St. John Thackeray, *Josephus: The Man and the Historian* (New York: Ktav, 1967), 5. See also Sterling, *Historiography and Self-Definition*, esp. 229-35.

among the Christians, Peregrinus was facetiously dubbed 'the new Socrates' (*Peregr.* 12).

h. *Socrates and Christian Apologetics*

Ernst Benz observes that Christian apologists were drawn to the figure of Socrates for three reasons. First, Christians increasingly viewed Christianity as the final and best philosophy in the Roman world. As such, the figure of Socrates became a type of proto-Christian philosopher. Secondly, Christians, who themselves faced judicial proceedings on account of their faith, found an ally in Socrates who was himself unjustly condemned for introducing new gods. Thirdly, Christians saw themselves as rejected martyr/prophets. As a result, they compared the rejection of the prophets in Jerusalem to the rejection of Socrates in Athens.[23]

To be sure, Platonic thought would come to influence many Christian theologians, so that Clement of Alexandria, for instance, would ask, 'What, after all, is Plato but Moses in Attic?' (*Stromata* 1.22.150). However, Christians regularly criticized much of what Socrates taught, including his negative view of the body and of bodily resurrection.[24] Though Christians did not always agree with Socrates' teaching, they were impressed by the manner in which he lived and died for what he held to be true. As Peter Ahrensdorf writes:

> What drew these Christians to Plato was above all the religious image that he left of the philosopher, an image which appealed to the core of the Christians' religious beliefs and passions, but not necessarily to their particular beliefs in particular doctrines.[25]

i. *Justin Martyr (110–165* CE*): Jesus as the New Socrates*

Justin Martyr, the first great early-church apologist, drew upon the story of Socrates in defense of the Christian faith. This is not surprising, given Justin's own philosophical inclinations. He was, as Benz notes, a philosopher, comparing one ancient philosopher (Socrates) to another (Christ).[26] For Justin, Socrates represented a pre-Christian manifestation of the λόγος. Justin was therefore keen to draw parallels between Socrates and Christians. For example, as evildoers accused

23. Ernst Benz, 'Christus und Sokrates in der alten Kirche', *ZNW* 43 (1951), 195-244.

24. See, for instance, Tertullian, *Apology* 46.

25. Peter J. Ahrensdorf, *The Death of Socrates and the Life of Philosophy: An Interpretation of Plato's Phaedo* (Albany: State University of New York Press, 1995), 204.

26. Benz, 'Christus und Sokrates in der alten Kirche', 198.

Socrates of introducing false gods, so also did they accuse Christians of religious error:

> And when Socrates endeavored, by true reason and examination, to bring these things to light, and deliver men from the demons, then the demons themselves, by means of men who rejoiced in iniquity, compassed his death, as an atheist and profane person, on the charge that he was introducing new divinities. (*1 Apol.* 5.4)

Then, in his *Second Apology*, Justin cites the injustice done to Socrates, an earnest man, who suffered persecution due to the influence of 'wicked demons' (2 *Apol.* 7). Again, Justin cites Socrates as an example of one who contemplated the Word (λόγος), and, as a result was unjustly accused of the same crime as the Christians: 'introducing new divinities' (2 *Apol.* 9).

j. *Tertullian (160–c. 220* CE*): 'What has Socrates to Do with Jesus?'*

In *A Treatise on the Soul* (c. 203), Tertullian often takes aim at Plato concerning the nature and existence of the soul. Tertullian opens the treatise with an extended discussion of the death of Socrates, and in doing so displays a detailed knowledge of Plato's account.[27] For Tertullian, Socrates is not a proto-Christian, but in fact an inconsistent philosopher who was plagued by a demon. Tertullian charges that Socrates' teachings on immortality were little more than the hope of a man 'unjustly condemned' (*On the Soul* 1.1). Christians, meanwhile, bore 'the unjust condemnation not of one city only, but of all the world'. Indeed, Socrates' hemlock was an easy death compared to Christians who endure 'every kind of bitter cruelty, on gibbets and in holocausts' (*On the Soul* 1.1). In his negative assessment of Socrates, Tertullian stands resolutely against the philosophically minded Justin. Yet, for both men the issue and manner of Socrates' death loomed large.

k. *Origen's* Contra Celsum*: Socrates vs. Jesus, Whose Death was Nobler?*

As an apologist, Origen (185–254 CE) also had to contend with those who charged that Jesus was 'bound in a most dishonorable fashion and executed most shamefully' (*Cels.* 6.10).[28] Celsus, in order to dis-

27. Tertullian in his argument refers to Socrates' imprisonment, the return of the ship from Delos, the hemlock draft, Socrates' tranquility, and Xanthippe's 'effeminate cry', namely, 'O Socrates, you are unjustly condemned' (*On the Soul* 1.1).

28. The translation for *Contra Celsum* is that of Frederick Crombie, as found in *The Ante-Nicene Fathers* (Grand Rapids: Eerdmans, 1885).

credit Origen's religion, aimed to demonstrate that Jesus did not measure up to the highest values of Greco-Roman virtues. One of Celsus' favorite tactics was to argue that Jesus' attitude towards death did not measure up to such prime Greco-Roman examples as Socrates.

Celsus' first accusation against Christians is that they were secretive, and therefore cowardly. Celsus charges that Jesus' disciples did not exhibit the courage of 'Socrates and his ilk', who 'encountered dangers for the sake of philosophy' (*Cels.* 1.3). Origen, in defense of Christian secretiveness, points out that while Athens repented for having prosecuted Socrates, Christians endured long-standing persecution. Origen further defends Christianity by noting that its founder, Jesus, also encountered many dangers for the sake of his teachings. As Socrates' death became a paradigm for noble suffering, Origen claims that Jesus became an example for others to follow. For the sake of humanity, Jesus encountered danger and suffered an inglorious death, so that he might inspire his followers to encounter dangers and 'embrace' death (*Cels.* 1.11).

Interestingly, Origen turns the tables on Celsus, invoking Socrates' death as an example against his opponent. Celsus charged that if Jesus were a god, or a prudent man, he would have avoided the events of the passion. Origen seizes the point to compare Jesus' voluntary death to that of Socrates:

> And yet Socrates knew that he would die after drinking the hemlock, and it was in his power, if he had allowed himself to be persuaded by Crito, by escaping from prison, to avoid these calamities; but nevertheless he decided, as it appeared to him consistent with right reason, that it was better for him to die as became a philosopher, than to retain his life in a manner unbecoming one. (*Cels.* 2.17)

Origen's argument demonstrates that he knew the Socrates story and that he could use it to defend the nobility of Jesus' death.

Jesus' agony in the garden would have been a potential stumbling-block for a Christian apologist who sought to present Jesus as one who faced death willingly and courageously. Celsus makes much of this fact, asking the following accusatory question:

> Why does he mourn and lament and pray to escape the fear of death, expressing himself in terms like these: 'Father, if it be possible, let this cup pass from me'? (*Cels.* 2.24)

Celsus sees this mournful prayer as evidence of Jesus' shameful unwillingness to obey God. Origen lamely replies that Celsus is 'grossly exaggerating the facts', and even goes on to say that 'it is nowhere found that Jesus lamented' (*Cels.* 2.24). Appearing to protest too loudly, Origen claims that Jesus demonstrated a 'cheerful obedience', in his willingness to drink the cup of suffering. Here it is hard to escape the conclusion that Origen's depiction of Jesus' death is more shaped by the story of Socrates, who 'seemed happy' upon meeting his death (Plato, *Phaedo* 58) than upon the Matthean account being discussed. Whether or not Origen wins the argument, it is clear that the noble death of Socrates loomed large in the minds of the ancients, and that the Christians would have to address the issue of how Jesus' death compared to it. We might here add that if Origen had made use of the Lukan passion, he would have had better ammunition against his pagan opponent. The Lukan Jesus does not mourn and lament as in Matthew. Furthermore, he appears far more willing to die.

4. *Evidence of the Socrates Story Elsewhere in Luke–Acts*

a. *The Significance of Finding Socrates in Luke–Acts*

Thus far, we have seen that the figure of Socrates, and especially the story of his death, loomed large in the ancient mind, and necessarily played a significant role in Jewish and early Christian apologetic literature. Not surprisingly, scholars contend that Luke knew and made use of the Socrates story elsewhere in Luke–Acts. This fact, if true, would make stronger the case for investigating the possible influence of the Socrates story on the passion narrative.

b. *Acts 5.29 and 4.19: The 'Socratic Tradition of Integrity'*

A clear instance of Socratic influence may be seen in the famous dictum of Peter standing before the Sanhedrin (Acts 5.29), and its parallel in Acts 4.19. As Gregory Sterling writes, 'Any student who has read the *Apology* of Plato can not fail to hear an echo in the apostles' retort to the Sanhedrin in Acts: πειθαρχεῖν δεῖ θεῷ μᾶλλον ἢ ἀνθρώποις'.[29] Indeed, Peter's words closely match those of Socrates before the Athenian council: μείσομαι δὲ πᾶλλον τῷ θεῷ ἢ ὑμῖν (*Apol.* 29D). Here Luke draws upon what Luke Johnson calls 'the Socratic tradition of integrity', according to which divine authority takes precedence over human opinion.[30] In fact, he takes what appears to be a

29. For acknowledgment of this parallel, see Conzelmann's *Acts of the Apostles*, 42.

30. Luke T. Johnson, *Acts of the Apostles* (Collegeville, MN: Liturgical Press, 1992), 81.

situational statement and turns it into a philosophical credo. This same Socratic tradition may be found in the Maccabean literature, where Eleazar chooses death over transgression of ancestral and divine law (2 Macc. 7.2; *4 Macc.* 5.16-38). However, Luke's wording is closer to Plato's account than to his Jewish-Hellenistic predecessors.

c. *Acts 17.16-34: Paul and Socrates*

Luke's familiarity with Hellenistic culture is clearly evident in the story of Paul at Athens. The speech itself, with judicial and deliberative elements, evidences Luke's knowledge of Greco-Roman rhetoric.[31] Likewise, Luke shows himself familiar with the history and culture of the day. Not only does the Lukan Paul (Acts 17.28) quote the Greek philosopher Aratus (*Phaenomena* 5), but he also displays basic knowledge of Stoic and Epicurean philosophy.[32] The passage also demonstrates, I will argue, Luke's knowledge of the most famous philosopher of all, Socrates.

For the ancients the very mention of Athens invoked historical memories of its greatest philosopher and the unjust death he died. Similarly, Socrates' name recalled the city's greatest achievement and most obvious failure. According to Josephus, Athens was renown as a city 'open' to all comers, yet closed to the wisdom and righteousness of its most famous inhabitant (*Apion* 2.262-65). Accordingly, Juvenal could offer up Athens as a parable against societal blindness to true virtue: 'O Athens, you had nothing better to offer than a cup of cold hemlock' (*Satires* 7.206). Evidence that the Socrates story remained part of the Athenian memory can be seen in the story of Phocion's unjust death, concerning which Plutarch comments:

> But Phocion's fate reminded the Greeks anew of that of Socrates; they felt that the sin and the misfortune of Athens were alike in both cases. (*Phoc.* 38.2)

Likewise, when Demonax was accused and put on trial in Athens, he was able to appeal to the Athenians' prior misjudgment of Socrates:

31. See Kennedy, *New Testament Interpretation*, 129-31; also see D. Zweck, 'The Exordium of the Areopagus Speech, Acts 17.22-23', *NTS* 35 (1989), 94-103; Soards, *Speeches in Acts*, 95-100; Karl Olav Sandnes, 'Paul and Socrates: The Aim of Paul's Areopagus Speech', *JSNT* 50 (1993), 13-26.

32. See, for instance, Jerome Neyrey, 'Acts 17, Epicureans and Theodicy: A Study in Stereotypes', in D. Balch and W. Meeks (eds.), *Greeks, Romans, and Christians: Essays in Honor of Abraham J. Malherbe* (Minneapolis: Fortress Press, 1990), 127-39.

> Men of Athens, you see me ready with my garland: come, sacrifice me like your former victim, for on that occasion your offering found no favour with the gods! (Lucian, *Demon.* 11)

Now, with the appearance of Paul, the Athenians were once more confronted with a critical choice. How would they treat the teacher of this new philosophy? Would they repeat their past mistake?

Scholars have seen in the Aeropagus speech striking parallels to the story of Socrates.[33] Karl Sandnes notes three basic similarities between Paul and Socrates.[34] First, the scene for Paul's and Socrates' activity in Athens is the market-place (ἀγορά) (Acts 17.17; *Apol.* 17C). Luke and Plato both employ the term ἐντυγχάνω, saying that Paul and Socrates talked to whomever they might chance upon (Acts 17.17). Secondly, the Socrates tradition is one of engaging in philosophical dialogue, often described by the verb διαλέγομαι.[35] Likewise, Paul engages in dialogue (διελέγετο) with some of 'the Epicurean and Stoic philosophers' (Acts 17.18).[36] In the LXX, the term may refer to a simple act of speaking (see 1 Esd. 8.46; Isa. 63), and elsewhere in the New Testament the term may simply refer to an address or lecture (see Heb. 12.5).[37] The presence of Stoics and Epicureans, however, points us to the philosophical coloring of the word. As Hans Conzelmann remarks, the dialogue 'awakens memories of Socrates'.[38] Thirdly, Paul and Socrates faced similar charges. Paul was accused of having introduced 'foreign gods' (ξένων δαιμονίων) (Acts 17.18). Socrates was charged with making 'new gods' (καινοὺς θεούς) (*Euth.* 3B) and with believing in 'new spiritual beings' (δαιμόνια καινά) (*Apol.* 24B). This part of the Socrates story was well known, appearing in the works of Xenophon, Diogenes, and the Christian apologist Justin.[39]

33. E. Benz remarks that Socrates appears here as 'first-born brother of the apostles' ('Christus und Sokrates in der alten Kirche', 207).

34. Sandnes, 'Paul and Socrates', 20-24.

35. Plato's *Euthyphro*, *Apology*, and *Phaedo* belong to the genre of dialogue. See also Xenophon's *Mem.* 2.10.1; Diogenes Laertius, *Lives* 2.20.45.122.

36. Paul elsewhere engages in such dialogue (διελέγετο) in the synagogue with Jews and Greeks (Acts 18.4), and again with Jews (18.19). A clearer instance of the philosophic coloring of the term can be found in the case of Paul 'engaging in dialogue (διαλεγόμενος) in the school (σχολῇ) of Tyrannus' (19.9)

37. See Gottlob Schrenk, 'διαλέγομαι', in *TDNT*, II, 93-95.

38. Conzelmann, *Acts of the Apostles*, 139.

39. See, e.g., Xenophon, *Mem.* 1.1.1.; Philostratus, *Life* 7.11; Justin Martyr, *2 Apol.* 10.5.

d. *Jesus as the First Christian Philosopher*
(1) *Christians as philosophers.* There is another piece of the puzzle which needs to be put in place, namely, Luke's presentation of Jesus himself as a type of Christian philosopher for the new school of Christian philosophy.

As we have seen already, Peter defended himself with words reminiscent of Socrates (Acts 4.19; 5.29), and Paul engaged in a type of philosophical dialogue with 'Epicurean and Stoic philosophers' (17.18). Furthermore, both Peter and Paul are known for their 'bold speech' (παρρησία) (2.29; 4.29, 31; 28.31). As Steve Mason notes, 'The mark of the true philosopher therefore was a determination to speak with *parrhesia* without regard for the consequences'.[40] This is exactly what we find among the early Christian preachers according to Luke.

Do we see evidence for Christianity as a type of philosophical school elsewhere in Acts? We may consider, for instance, the idyllic portrayal of the Christian community (Acts 2.44-45; 4.32-35), which recalls the legendary followers of Pythagoras, as well as Josephus's Essenes, and Philo's Therapeutae.[41] In their communal sharing, these first Christians were following the prescriptions of their movement's founding philosopher who had much to say about the negative influence of wealth (i.e. Lk. 6.20-26; 12.13-21; 14.1-14; 16.19-31). We also note that Christianity is explicitly labeled, albeit derisively, a philosophical school: 'the school (αἱρέσεως) of the Nazarenes' (Acts 24.5; also 24.14; 28.22).

Does Luke present Jesus in such a way that the Hellenistic audience would have recognized him as a philosopher? We have evidence of this especially in his employment of the symposium genre.

(2) *Symposium as Greco-Roman literary convention.* The symposia of Plato and Xenophon mark the beginning of a genre which remained a vibrant literary form up to Luke's own day, as evidenced by Plutarch's symposia, *Dinner of the Seven Wise Men* and *Table Talk*. At first, the symposia were written by the Socratics as a means to preserve and communicate the wisdom of their teacher. Later, symposia were composed to depict well-known personages as wise in the tradition of Socrates, the prototypical philosopher. The symposia literature

40. Steve Mason, *Josephus and the New Testament* (Peabody, MA: Hendrickson, 1957), 219.

41. See Josephus, *War* 2.122-23; *Ant.* 18.18-22; Philo, *Prob.* 75–87; *Contempl.* 16. For discussion of Hellenistic parallels, see P.W. van der Horst, 'Hellenistic Parallels to the Acts of the Apostles', *JSNT* 25 (1985), 59-60.

finds its way into Jewish circles, especially in its apologetic literature. For instance, the Hellenized Philo remarked that the banquets of Plato and Xenophon were 'models of a happily conducted banquet', with which the meals of the Therapeutae compared more than favorably (*Contemp.* 57). *The Letter of Aristeas* employs the symposium genre within a larger literary framework.[42] The symposium here serves the literary function of highlighting the wisdom of the LXX's translators.[43]

(3) *The structure of a symposium*. The general structure of the symposium includes (1) a host's invitation, (2) a *fait divers*, that is, an incident which leads to a question or dialogue, and is followed by (3) a learned discourse.[44] The symposium as a genre furnishes the setting for learned discourse and further highlights the wisdom of the invited guest(s). Josef Martin demonstrated that the symposium genre consists of certain topoi, including a predictable cast of characters and situations.[45] E. Springs Steele, in a helpful distillation of Martin's work, informs us that the situational topoi of a typical symposium include (1) a wealthy, prominent, or wise host, (2) a chief guest, known especially for wisdom, (3) other guests of high social status. The symposium especially highlights the wit and wisdom of its invited guest(s).[46] This function is especially clear in the symposia of Xenophon and Plato, who use the genre to pass on the wisdom of Socrates. Likewise, this function serves an apologetic purpose in *Aristeas*, so that the author is able to demonstrate that the Jewish translators of the LXX are fully versed in the philosophic wisdom of the day.

(4) *Typical topics for discussion at a symposium*. While the symposium is characterized by the discussion of a whole range of topics, a number of themes are quite common. In Plutarch's *Table Talk*, such topics as

42. See Moses Hadas, *Aristeas to Philocrates* (New York: Ktav, 1951), 42-43.

43. For a further discussion of the symposium's influence on Jewish culture, see Siegfried Stein, 'The Influence of Symposia Literature on the Literary Form of the Pesah Haggada', *JJS* 8 (1957), 13-44.

44. E. Springs Steele, 'Luke 11.37-54 – A Modified Hellenistic Symposium?', *JBL* 103 (1984), 379-94.

45. For the classic scholarly work on symposia, see Josef Martin's *Symposion: Die Geschichte einer literarischen Form* (Studien zur Geschichte und Kultur des Altertums, 17/1-2; Paderborn: Schöningh, 1931).

46. J. Delobel ('L'onction par la pécheresse', *ETL* 42 [1966], 415-75 [459]), argues that the symposium furnishes a setting in which the author may highlight the wisdom of the honored guest(s).

(1) meal etiquette, (2) types of food or wine, and (3) ethics/wisdom are declared subjects fit for discussion.

Under the subject heading of meal etiquette, the topic of order and status at table is typically discussed. In Plato's *Symposium*, there is discussion as to who will have the honor of reclining next to Agathon, as well as who will sit next to Socrates. Similarly, in Plutarch's *Dinner*, a certain Alexidemus is insulted by his poor place at table, upon which he is told that such objections are an insult to host and guest alike. Again in *Table Talk*, the participants argue that good order is necessary for pleasant dining. Nor is this motif neglected in *Letter of Aristeas*, in which the arrangement of couches is described as a means to honor the Israelite men, whose positions at table were ordered according to seniority (*Aristeas* 183, 187).

Again, it is common to find discussion concerning the food and drink served at table. Thus, in *Dinner*, the question arises as to which guests should receive the best food, and in *Table Talk*, there is a discussion as to why three or five drinks are more healthy than four. Again, in *Aristeas* the symposium affords an opportunity to speak about the wisdom of taking food and drink in moderation (*Aristeas* 223).

Yet, whatever the topic at hand, the Symposium provided a setting for the sharing of wisdom. When asked 'How ought one conduct himself in banquets (συμποσίων)', one of the wise translators of the LXX answered, 'One ought invite lovers of learning and men capable of suggesting what may be useful to the realm and the lives of its subjects—much more harmonious and sweeter music you could not find' (*Aristeas* 286-87). Thus, the symposium was a place to share food and to highlight the wisdom of the philosopher.

(5) *Luke's presentation of Jesus as philosopher at symposia*. Luke makes use of the symposium genre in no less than four pericopes: Lk. 5.29-39; 7.36-50; 11.37-54; and 14.1-24. These pericopes follow the typical order of a symposium and contain standard topics for discussion. Each meal follows the typical pattern for the symposium genre: (1) a setting at a banquet (5.29; 7.36; 11.37; 14.1), (2) a *fait divers* (5.29: 7.37-38; 11.38; 14.2-6), (3) reaction (5.30; 7.39; 11.38; 14.2-6), (4) Jesus' response (5.31-32; 7.40-48; 11.44; 14.7-14), (5) a further question or statement (5.35; 7.49; 11.45; 14.15), and (6) Jesus' response (5.34-39; 7.50; 11.46-52; 14.16-24).[47] Likewise, Luke's symposia contain the standard topics for discussion, such as (1) meal etiquette (5.30; 7.44-46;

47. See Sterling's *Historiography and Self-Definition*, 370.

11.38; 14.8-14), (2) types of food or wine (5.36-38; 14.16), and (3) ethics (5.31-32; 7.37-47; 11.39-52; 14.13-14).

Luke, alone among the Gospel writers, has consciously appropriated the Greco-Roman genre of the symposium. His use of the symposium genre serves to highlight Jesus' wisdom and to claim Jesus' rightful place as a philosopher of great wisdom. Here we concur with Steele, who sees Luke's editorial hand at work, with the result that 'Jesus is portrayed as a wisdom teacher, a sage, as was Socrates by Plato and Xenophon'.[48]

5. *The Socrates Story: Primary Motifs*

a. *Introduction*

If Luke drew upon the Socrates story to paint his pictures of Peter and Paul, we do well to ask whether Luke also drew upon Socratic motifs to shape his passion narrative. This apologetic strategy had been previously employed by the Hellenistic–Jewish authors of the Maccabean literature, and played a prominent part in second-century Christian apologetic literature. What better way could Luke take away the shame of the cross than to link Jesus' death to that of Socrates? At this point, it would be helpful to review essential aspects of the story of Socrates' death.

b. *Socrates Dies as a Righteous Man*

For Plato, even if a man dies terribly, he is blessed, provided that he is righteous: 'The righteous man (ὁ δίκαιος), though stretched on a rack, though his eyes are dug out, will be happy' (*Republic* 2.5). Socrates himself says that a man, adorned with righteousness (δικαιοσύνη), should face death cheerfully (*Phaedo* 114E). Fittingly, Plato ends the *Phaedo* with this summary judgment of Socrates: 'Such was the end, Echecrates, of our friend, who was, as we may say, of all those of his time whom we have known, the best and wisest and most righteous man (δικαιοτάτου)' (*Phaedo* 118).

As we have seen, the chief obligations of righteousness include duty to God and country. Accordingly, Socrates said a prayer as he received the executioner's poison: 'But I may and must pray to the gods that my departure hence be a fortunate one; so I offer this prayer, and may it be granted' (*Phaedo* 117C). Socrates' duty to God will be made clearer in his understanding that his death is a necessity brought by God. This will be an important theme of the Lukan

48. Springs Steele, 'Luke 11.37-54', 393.

narrative as well, as we shall see. A second part of righteousness is duty to one's country which, we will see below, Socrates takes great pains to fulfill. Here, we simply note that Socrates praised the fatherland as something to be esteemed more honorable (τιμιώτερον), precious (σεμνότερον), and holy (ἁγιώτερον) than even parents and ancestors (*Crito* 51B).

Finally, we may add that Plato's assessment of Socrates himself as a virtuous and righteous man is echoed by Xenophon, who ends his memoirs with an encomiastic flourish:

> For myself, I have described him as he was: so religious that he did nothing without counsel from the gods; so just (δίκαιος) that he did no injury, however small, to any man, but conferred the greatest benefits on all who dealt with him; so self-controlled that he never chose the pleasanter rather than the better course... To me then he seemed to be all that a truly good and happy man must be. If there is any doubter, let him set the character of other men beside these things; then let him judge. (*Mem.* 4.8.2)

Socrates embodies the virtues, especially piety and righteousness.

c. *The Injustice of Socrates' Sentence*
An essential part of the Socrates story is the fact that the sage was an innocent victim of an unjust sentence (κρίσιν ἄδικον) (*Apol.* 41B). According to his accusers, Socrates had committed injustice (ἀδικεῖ) by virtue of his teaching (*Apol.* 19B). However, this was clearly a false accusation (διαβολή) (*Apol.* 19B; 21B). Socrates' opponents had, in fact, 'told many lies (ἐψεύσαντο)' about him (*Apol.* 1A), saying 'little or nothing true' (οὐδὲν ἀληθές) (*Apol.* 1B). Moreover, Socrates argued, most people knew this to be true because he had taught openly among them (see *Apol.* 19D).

d. *Socrates' Death as a Necessity Brought by God*
Understanding his death to be a matter of divine necessity, Socrates told his friends, 'It is not unreasonable to say that a man must not kill himself until God sends some necessity (ἀνάγκην) upon him, such as has now come upon me' (*Phaedo* 62C). Indeed, Socrates understood his entire life of philosophy as having been commanded by God:

> But as I believe, as I have been commanded to do this by god through oracles and dreams and in every way in which any man was ever commanded by divine power to do anything whatsoever. (*Apol.* 33C)

Socrates, in his defense, claimed that if ever he embarked on a course which the gods opposed, his prophetic monitor would alert him (*Apol.* 40A). This sign, according to Socrates, was divine (τὸ τοῦ θεοῦ σημεῖον) (*Apol.* 40B), and something to which he was accustomed (τὸ εἰωθὸς σημεῖον) (*Apol.* 40C).[49]

Concerned with the opinion of God rather than the public, he compared himself to an athlete who pays attention not to the crowds, but to the physician or trainer (*Crito* 47B). Therefore, Socrates accepted his death, for, as he says, 'This is where God leads us' (*Crito* 54E). Consequently, Socrates understood his death not as something to be feared or avoided, but as a necessity: 'It would be absurd if at my age I were disturbed because I must (δεῖ) die now' (*Crito* 43C; see 44A). As such, Socrates displays his righteousness by means of obedience.

e. *Socrates' Refusal to Escape and his Obedience to the Law*

Socrates' friends encouraged him to escape, arguing that the Athenians were acting unjustly (*Crito* 45E). Nevertheless, Socrates rejected the idea. Why? Andrew Woozley argues that Socrates refused to escape because the 'consequences of disobedience are, or would be, socially destructive'.[50] However, it appears that Socrates concerned himself not so much with the question of what would happen to society by escaping and setting a bad precedent, but whether the act of escaping, in and of itself, was just:

> Then we agree that the question is whether it is right (δίκαιον) for me to try to escape from here without the permission of the Athenians, or not right (οὐ δίκαιον). And if it appears to be right (δίκαιον), let us try it, and if not, let us give it up. (*Crito* 48C)

Thus, Socrates would base his decision on justice, not expedience.

According to Socrates, '[T]he law must be obeyed' (*Crito* 19A). This obedience is not blind to injustice, but an allegiance owed to the government. Socrates reminds his friends that as a citizen of Athens he has entered into a social contract with the *polis* which, like a parent, nurtured and educated him (see *Crito* 50D). As Andrew Barker writes, 'It [i.e. escape] would be ἄδικον because, regardless of its consequences, it would constitute a voluntary breach of agreement and a deliberate abrogation of the rights and functions of the πόλις'.[51] Indeed, Socrates claimed that greater allegiance was owed to the country than even to one's parents:

49. As to the exact nature of this sign, the ancients themselves debated. See Plutarch, *The Sign of Socrates*.

50. Anthony D. Woozley, 'Socrates on Disobeying the Law', in G. Vlastos (ed.), *The Philosophy of Socrates* (New York: Macmillan, 1972), 299.

51. Andrew Barker, 'Why Did Socrates Refuse to Escape?', *Phronesis* 22 (1977), 13-28 (27).

> Or is your wisdom such that you do not see that your country is more precious and more to be revered and is holier and in higher esteem among the gods and among men of understanding than your mother and your father and all your ancestors, and that you ought to show to her more reverence and obedience and humility when she is angry than to your father, and ought either to convince her by persuasion or to do whatever she commands, and to suffer, if she commands you to suffer, in silence, and if she orders you to be scourged or imprisoned or if she leads you to war to be wounded or slain, her will is to be done, and this is right, and you must not give way or draw back or leave your post, but in war and in court and everywhere, you must do whatever the state, your country, commands, or must show her by persuasion what is really right (δίκαιον), but that it is impious to use violence against either your father or mother, and much more impious to use it against your country? (*Crito* 51B-C)

Socrates' allegiance to the country is not blind. He recognizes that the individual may have legitimate grievances. However, the just man will use no violence against the state, for he knows that the state is dear to the gods.

f. *Not Requiting Evil with Evil*

For Socrates, it is especially incumbent upon the individual not to retaliate against the unjust acts of the state with further acts of injustice. In this vein, he asks Crito, 'Well then, is it right to requite evil with evil?' (*Crito* 49C). When Crito agrees that retaliation is unjust, Socrates continues, 'Then we ought neither to requite wrong with wrong nor to do evil to anyone, no matter what he may have done to us' (*Crito* 49C).

For Socrates, an unjust action is never made just by the injustice of another. He argues forcefully against situational ethics:

> Are we to say that we should in no way do wrong, or that we should do wrong under some conditions and not others? Is it not true that wrongdoing is never in any way good or fine, as we have often agreed in the past? (*Crito* 50A)

Indeed, it is essential for the virtuous man to be willing to endure suffering rather than commit wrong, for wrongdoing is wrong in every situation: 'And whether we must endure still more grievous sufferings than these, or lighter ones, is not wrongdoing inevitably an evil and a disgrace to the wrongdoer?' (*Crito* 50B). As such, Socrates' teaching allowed for no retaliation, even if one's cause was just.

g. *The Courage of Socrates*

Socrates displayed remarkably quiet courage during his final days. He attributed this to the fact that he knew he was going to the gods, who are 'good masters' (*Phaedo* 64C). As Socrates told his judges, 'I think a man who has really spent his life in philosophy is naturally of good courage (θαρρεῖν) when he is to die' (*Phaedo* 64A). Describing the philosopher's countenance, Phaedo says: '[H]e seemed to me to be happy (εὐδαίμων), both in his bearing and his words, he was meeting death so fearlessly (ἀδεῶς) and nobly (γενναίως)' (*Phaedo* 58E). The executioner likewise noticed the quiet courage of Socrates, saying, 'No, I have found you in all this time in every way the noblest (γενναιότατον) and gentlest (πραότατον) and best (ἄριστον) man who has ever come here' (*Phaedo* 116C). This courage and serenity comes to the foreground in the manner in which Socrates receives the poison:

> At the same time he held out the cup to Socrates. He took it, and very gently (ἵλεως), Echecrates, without trembling or changing colour or expression... (*Phaedo* 117B)

Courageous man that he is, Socrates remains in control of himself and maintains a placid demeanor, even in dying.

h. *Socrates is 'Trained' for Death*

Part of the reason Socrates is able to face death willingly, even cheerfully, is that he has been 'trained' for it.[52] Socrates' willingness to die was the result of preparation and practice. Concerning one's attitude towards death, Socrates concludes:

> It would be absurd if a man who had been all his life fitting himself (παρασκευάζονθ') to live as nearly in a state of death as he could, should then be disturbed when death came to him. (*Phaedo* 67E)

According to Socrates, 'true philosophers practice (μελετῶσι) dying, and death is less terrible to them than to others' (*Phaedo* 67E). In the *Crito*, Socrates explicitly compares the virtuous life to that of an athlete, who ignores the opinions of the people, and listens only to his trainer [God]:

> And he must act (πρακτέον) and exercise (γυμναστέον) and eat and drink as the one man who is his director and who knows the business thinks best rather than as all the others think. (*Crito* 47C)

Socrates was ready and able to die, because he had prepared himself as an athlete, exercising and training in virtue, according to the will of God.[53] Moreover, part of this training is to concern oneself with the

52. On Socrates' readiness to die, see Ahrensdorf, *The Death of Socrates*, esp. 35-37.

53. Commenting on Socrates' athletic training in virtue, Xenophon writes, 'He was not only the most rigid of all men in the government of his passions and

praise of God rather than that of man: 'Then he ought to fear the blame and welcome the praise of that one man [i.e. God] and not of the multitude' (*Crito* 47B).

i. *The Role of Friends/Noble Grief*

A special feature of the Socrates story is the role which his friends played at his death. The presence of grieving friends, as John Kloppenborg writes, 'underscores the great affection that disciples have for their teacher and affords the sage another opportunity to teach'.[54] The significance of the friends is seen in the question of Echecrates, near the beginning of the dialogue, in which he asks:

> What took place at his death, Phaedo? What was said and done? And which of his friends were with him? Or did the authorities forbid them to be present, so that he died without friends (φίλων)? (*Phaedo* 58C)

To the question of whether Socrates died without friends, Phaedo replied, 'Not at all. Some were there, in fact, a good many' (*Phaedo* 58C).[55] Socrates was accompanied by those who call him 'friend' (*Phaedo* 118). As friends offer questions, Socrates teaches about death and dying. The friends' loyalty further serves to highlight Socrates' goodness.

The friends demonstrate their affection especially in tears. Plato describes the moment when Socrates receives the poison:

> Up to that time most of us had been able to restrain our tears fairly well, but when we watched him drinking and saw that he had drunk the poison, we could do so no longer, but in spite of myself, my tears rolled down in floods, so that I wrapped my face in my cloak and wept for myself; for it was not for him that I wept, but for my own misfortune of being deprived of a friend. Crito had got up and gone away even before I did, because he could not restrain his tears. But Apollodorus, who had been weeping all the time before, then wailed aloud in his grief and made us all break down, except Socrates himself. But he said, 'What conduct is this, you strange men! I sent the women away chiefly for this very reason, that they might not behave in this absurd way; for I have heard that it is best to die in silence. Keep quiet and be brave.' Then we were ashamed and controlled our tears. (*Phaedo* 117C-E)

Socrates gently chides his followers for their weeping. Tears, however, also signal the loyalty of those who mourn. Thus, the weeping

appetites, but also most able to withstand cold, heat, and every kind of labor' (*Mem.* 1.2.1).

54. Kloppenborg, '"Exitus clari viri"', 114.

55. The group included Echecrates, Phaedo, Apollodorus, Cebes, Simmias, and Crito.

of Socrates' friends serves three purposes: (1) it demonstrates the loyalty of the disciples; (2) it accents Socrates' worthiness (i.e. tears are not shed for an ignoble man); and (3) it points us to Socrates' own calm courage. That tears serve this function in Socrates, we see in the story of the executioner who 'burst into tears' when he was about to administer the poison. Commenting on the guard's tears, Socrates says:

> How charming the man is! Ever since I have been here he has been coming to see me and talking with me from time to time, and has been the best of men, now how nobly (γενναίως) he weeps for me! (*Phaedo* 117B)

j. *Socrates' Wife: A Woman's Grief*

Weeping serves a similar function in the depiction of Xanthippe, Socrates' wife. Xanthippe visited her husband Socrates on the morning of his execution, and acted according to the ancients' stereotype of grieving women:

> Now when Xanthippe saw us, she cried out and said the kind of thing that women always do say, 'Oh Socrates, this is the last time now that your friends will speak to you or you to them'. (*Phaedo* 60A)

At this outburst, members of Crito's entourage took her away, 'wailing and beating her breast' (*Phaedo* 60A). Given Xanthippe's limited role in the account, her weeping is surely not recounted in order to demonstrate her weakness.[56] Instead, Plato illustrates the fact that Socrates receives the customary lament of women. Further, Xanthippe's weeping provides a convenient contrast to Socrates' own calm serenity and wisdom.[57]

k. *Prophecy of Retribution*

In death, Socrates becomes a prophet of retribution, predicting that he would be honored after his death, and that those who punished him would themselves be punished and shamed.

> And now I wish to prophesy to you, O ye who have condemned me; for I am now at the time when men most do prophesy, the time just before death. And I say to you, ye men who have slain me, that punishment will come upon you straightway after my death, far more grievous in sooth than the punishment of death which you have meted out to me. (*Apol.* 39C)

56. She appears only here, and later, as part of the family (see *Phaedo* 116B).

57. For a discussion of Xanthippe's lack of comprehension, see Thomas L. Pangle, 'Socrates in Xenophon's Political Writings', in Paul A. Vander Waerdt (ed.), *The Socratic Movement* (Ithaca, NY: Cornell University Press), 127-50 (143-44).

The punishment, Socrates says, will come from the young, who will prove very critical of those who condemned him (*Apol.* 39C).[58]

6. *Socrates as a Possible Source for the Lukan Passion: Summary*

Within this chapter, we have seen the pervasive influence of the Socrates story within the Greco-Roman world. Attaining almost canonical status, the story of Socrates' death is recounted by the popular philosophers, became a mainstay of popular literature, and was passed on through the educational system. The philosopher's death finds its way into Jewish apologetic literature, as evidenced by the Maccabean literature as well as Josephus. Likewise, Socrates becomes a major talking point in the Christian apologetic literature, including the writings of Justin Martyr, Tertullian, and Origen.

I have isolated a number of motifs of which the story of Socrates is comprised. I noted that he died as a righteous man and that he was unjustly put to death. Seeing that his death was a necessity brought by God, Socrates refused to escape, obeying the law, and not requiting evil for evil. In particular, we observed Socrates' courage, made possible by the fact that he was, in fact, 'trained for death'. His friends grieved over him, as did his wife. Socrates, though, was not concerned for himself, but predicted that retribution would come upon the city. Of these motifs, a number seem especially significant for our discussion of Luke. We will be especially concerned with the fact that Jesus, like Socrates, faced death as a righteous and courageous man who saw his death as part of the divine necessity. We will also note the grief of Jesus' friends.

There are good reasons for suspecting that Luke could have made use of the Socrates story to color his own picture of Jesus' death. As a literate and knowledgeable writer, Luke most likely would have been familiar with the Socrates story. Indeed, we have seen that the figure of Socrates casts its shadow elsewhere in Luke–Acts. We see Socrates in Peter's statements of integrity (Acts 4.19; 5.29) as well as in Paul's Areopagus speech. We also have evidence that Luke aimed to present Christianity as a type of philosophy, of which Jesus was the founder, and Peter and Paul were major proponents. All of this evidence suggests that Luke would have had the means and the motive to color the passion narrative with the story of Socrates.

58. This prediction that posterity will judge the accusers harshly and Socrates well is repeated by Xenophon, who records the words of Socrates, 'But now, if I am to die unjustly, they who unjustly kill me will bear the shame of it' (*Mem.* 4.8.9).

4

THE JEWISH MARTYROLOGICAL TRADITION AND THE LUKAN PASSION

1. *Introduction*

In this chapter we will examine Hellenistic–Jewish martyrological literature as a possible resource for Luke's presentation of Jesus' death. As we shall see, a number of the features of Hellenistic–Jewish martyrdom reflect what we have seen in the noble death tradition and the death of Socrates.

W.H.C. Frend has forcefully argued that the idea of religious martyrdom was not known in the Greco-Roman world.[1] Frend acknowledged Judean parallels to the Greco-Roman materials, but noted significant differences. Jewish martyrdom carries with it notions of expiatory sacrifices, and presents the martyr's death as a witness to God's mighty works.[2] Greco-Roman 'martyrdom', Frend argues, owes more to reason than religion.

Yet, from what we have seen in Greco-Roman rhetoric and the story of Socrates, I would contend that Frend's distinction may be overdrawn. As it stands, much of the martyrological material overlaps with, and indeed draws from, motifs found in Greco-Roman rhetoric. The same is also true of the philosopher's death, of which Socrates is the prime example.[3] However, the martyrological literature has its own distinct motifs, and presumably may have mediated certain Greco-Roman notions of a praiseworthy death to an author such as Luke. As data for comparison, I will use the Maccabean

1. W.H.C. Frend, *Martyrdom and Persecution in the Early Church: A Study of a Conflict from the Maccabees to Donatus* (Oxford: Oxford University Press, 1965), 31-68.

2. Frend, *Martyrdom and Persecution*, 66-67. See also Zeph Stewart, 'Greek Crowns and Christian Martyrs', in Patrick Cramer (ed.), *Mémorial André-Jean Festugière* (Geneva: Genève Press, 1984), 119-24 (120).

3. See Seeley, *The Noble Death*, 83-143.

literature, especially 2 and *4 Maccabees*, as well as Josephus' description of the Essenes (*War* 2.151-53; see also 1.648-55).

2. *Martyrdom and Luke:* Status Quaestionis

Martin Dibelius stands among the first commentators to view the Lukan Passion as an attempt to portray Jesus' death as a martyrdom:

> The Suffering Saviour is the Man of God who is attacked by evil powers and who, with His patience and forgiveness, is a model of innocent suffering. Luke regards these events in the place where he consequently puts them not as the completion of salvation, but as the story of a saintly man closely united with God. The literary consequence of this view is that Luke presents the Passion as a martyrdom.[4]

The martyr thesis has been taken up by Conzelmann and Talbert among others.[5] H.W. Surkau, in his study of early Christian martyrdom, places the Lukan passion narrative firmly within the Jewish martyrological tradition.[6]

The influence of Jewish martyrological literature on early Christian interpretations of Jesus' death has been explored most thoroughly by E. Lohse in *Märtyrer und Gottesknecht*.[7] Lohse argues that Jewish/Palestinian martyrological literature influenced Christians in their understanding of Jesus' death as vicarious. The martyr thesis, as applied to the Lukan passion, has been widely challenged on the grounds that it neglects Luke's theology of atonement. In response, Fitzmyer and Brown, among others, have argued that Luke makes use of martyrological motifs, but not to the exclusion of other themes.[8] Such an understanding permits us to ask what martyrological motifs may be found in the Lukan passion.

4. Dibelius, *From Tradition to Gospel*, 201.
5. See Hans Conzelmann, *The Theology of St. Luke* (London: Macmillan, 1960), 83-89. See, more recently, Charles Talbert, *Reading Luke: A Literary and Theological Commentary on the Third Gospel* (New York: Crossroad, 1982), esp. 212-18.
6. H.W. Surkau, *Martyrien in jüdischer und frühchristlicher Zeit* (Göttingen: Vandenhoeck & Ruprecht, 1938), 82-105.
7. E. Lohse, *Märtyrer und Gottesknecht* (Göttingen: Vandenhoeck & Ruprecht, 1955).
8. Fitzmyer, *Luke*, II, 1367. Other scholars who have made much of the martyrological themes in Luke include A. Feuillet, *L'Agonie de Gethsemani: Enquête exégétique et théologique suivie d'une étude du 'Mystère de Jésus' de Pascal* (Paris: J. Gabalda, 1977); J.W. Holleran, *The Synoptic Gethsemane* (Rome: Gregorian University Press, 1973); J. Massyngbaerde Ford, *My Enemy is my Guest: Jesus and Violence in Luke* (Maryknoll, NY: Orbis Books, 1984), esp. 118-21.

Brown briefly summarizes what he sees as the martyrological aspects of the Lukan passion: (1) emphasis on Jesus' innocence; (2) emphasis on Jesus' suffering as a just and holy person; (3) description of Jesus' death as a 'baptism by fire' (12.49-53); (4) Jesus' struggle against great powers (i.e. kings, rulers, and Satan); (5) and the parallels which Luke draws between the deaths of Jesus and Stephen.[9] To be sure, these and other aspects of martyrdom do appear in the Lukan narrative. Yet, we will ask, on what martyrological sources, if any, does Luke draw for his portrayal?

3. *Types of Martyrdom in the Ancient World*

Charles Talbert has argued that different streams of martyrdom ran side-by-side in the ancient world.[10] The Greco-Roman world had its own type of martyrological literature, epitomized in the writings of such popular philosophers as Seneca and Epictetus.[11] Here we think of Seneca's *Epistle* 24, in which he recounts the noble deaths of Rutilius, Metellus, Socrates, Mucius, and Cato (*Ep.* 24.3-6). Likewise, the Old Testament includes any number of stories of prophets dying at the hands of God's people (see Jer. 2.20; Neh. 9.26; 1 Kgs 10.10; 2 Chron. 24.20-22; see also Mt. 23.31-39; Mk 12.1-12).[12] Most commentators argue that Luke depicted Jesus as a martyr according to this Jewish Old Testament type, which includes Abel, Zechariah, and the prophets of old (see Lk. 6.23; 11.47-51; 13.34).[13] The main motif of this type of Old Testament martyr is that God's prophet has been rejected by his people. Surely, this motif is present in Luke's Gospel.[14]

There is yet another stream of martyrdom which I will examine more closely, namely, Hellenistic–Jewish martyrdom as evidenced in the Maccabean literature and the writings of Josephus. The Maccabean literature and the writings of Josephus are noteworthy because they, like the third Gospel, are the products of authors who are thoroughly rooted in both the Jewish and Hellenistic worlds.[15] As

9. See Brown, *Death of the Messiah*, I, 31-32.
10. See Talbert, 'Martyrdom and the Lukan Social Ethic', 103-106.
11. See Seeley, *The Noble Death*, esp. 113-41.
12. See Talbert, 'Martyrdom and the Lukan Social Ethic', 104.
13. For a discussion of Jesus as prophet/martyr according to the Old Testament type, see H. Aschermann, 'Zum Agoniegebet Jesu, Luk. 22,43-44', *ThViat* 5 (1953–54), 143-49.
14. For a summary of Luke's Prophet Christology, see Just, *Luke*, 184-88.
15. For a discussion of the similarities between Luke–Acts, the Maccabean literature, and the writings of Josephus, see Aune's *The New Testament in its Literary*

Jan Willem van Henten notes, Jewish-Hellenistic martyrdoms share the following common elements:[16]

1. pagan authorities issue a decree, in a situation of oppression, which carries a death penalty;
2. the content of the decree makes it impossible for Jews to stay faithful to their God, the Law, and their Jewish way of life;
3. when Jews are forced to decide between complying with the decree or remaining faithful to their religion and their practice, they choose to die rather than obey the authorities;
4. this decision becomes obvious during the examination, which is sometimes accompanied by tortures;
5. the execution is described.

Clearly, this pattern does not fit Luke's passion narrative closely enough to label it a martyrdom, per se. In Luke's passion Jesus is not put on trial for defying a Roman decree, but because he has enemies among the Jewish authorities themselves (Lk. 23.2-4). However, we can see how the martyrological literature could have appealed to the author of Luke–Acts. Luke, like Josephus and the authors of the Maccabean literature, had certain apologetic concerns. Luke aimed to demonstrate that his Jewish subject was in fact noble and praiseworthy according to well-known Greco-Roman standards. Therefore, we will investigate how the martyrological literature may have been used as a tool to paint the picture of Jesus as a godly man who suffers an unjust death.

4. *Characteristics of Hellenistic–Jewish Martyrdom*

At this point, we do well to investigate the essential features of Hellenistic–Jewish martyrdom, especially as it relates to the topic of the noble or praiseworthy death. By singling out the basic features of these martyr stories, we will be able to compare them to the Lukan passion and ask whether and to what extent Luke drew upon them for his own depiction of Jesus' death.

a. *Martyrdom as a Contest for Virtue and Victory*

Alois Stöger sees martyrdom essentially as a contest between the forces of good and evil.[17] In this contest, the martyr struggles to act

Environment, 77-115. For a comparison between Luke–Acts and Josephus, see Sterling, *Historiography and Self-Definition*, esp. 227-393.

16. See van Henten, *The Maccabean Martyrs*, 8.

virtuously in the face of temptation unto death. By overcoming evil forces, the fallen martyr is declared victor in the contest. 2 Maccabees 14.37-46, for instance, specifically calls Razis's death an ἀγών. As van Henten writes, the passage 'conveys the impression of a contest between this pious Jew and the Seleucid soldiers'.[18] The chief Seleucid antagonist, Nicanor, sought to arrest Razis in the hope of dealing the Jewish people a 'hard blow' (2 Macc. 14.40). Razis, in the tradition of the noble death, chose 'to die nobly' rather than 'fall into the hands of vile men and suffer outrages unworthy of his noble birth' (2 Macc. 14.42). Razis's determination not to be captured recalls Aristotle's praise for the man who does 'not allow himself to be beaten' (*Rhet.* 1.9.24). Though Razis dies, he is victorious in the struggle for virtue.

4 Maccabees offers a more extensive picture of martyrdom as a contest between good and evil. In this contest, Antiochus plays the role of the evil tempter, urging the Maccabean martyrs, 'Eat of the swine flesh and save yourself' (*4 Macc.* 5.6). The martyrs, on the other hand, are compared to athletes engaged in a noble contest (γενναῖος ὁ ἀγών) for virtue (16.16). Having received training in the law of God (5.23-24; 13.22), they defend this law with 'their own blood and noble sweat' (ἰδίῳ αἵματι καὶ γενναίῳ ἱδρῶτι) (7.8). Likewise, we are told that Eleazar faced death like 'a noble athlete' (γενναῖος ἀθλητής), with 'his face bathed in sweat' (ἱδρῶν γέ τοι τὸ πρόσωπον) (6.10, 11). These descriptions, we shall see, will be important in our discussion of Jesus' own struggle on the Mount of Olives.

In an extended metaphor, the author of 4 Maccabees casts the martyrdoms entirely in terms of an athletic contest:

> Divine indeed was the contest (ἀγών) of which they were the issue. Of that contest virtue was the umpire (ἠθλοθέτει); and its score (δοκιμάζουσα) was for constancy. Victory (νῖκος) was incorruptibility in a life of long duration. Eleazar was the prime contestant (προηγωνίζετο); but the mother of the seven sons entered the competition, and the brothers too vied for the prize (ἠγωνίζοντο). The tyrant was the adversary (ἀντηγωνίζετο), and the world and humanity were the spectators (ἐθεώρει). Reverence for God was the winner, and crowned her own athletes (ἀθλητὰς στεφανοῦσα). Who did not marvel at the athletes (ἀθλητάς) of divine legislation, who were not astonished by them? (*4 Macc.* 17.11-16)

The vocabulary of the athletic contest (ἀγών) pervades the passage. The martyrs are athletes (ἀθλητής) engaged in a contest. Eleazar

17. Alois Stöger, 'Eigenart und Botschaft der lukanischen Passiongeschichte', *BK* 24 (1969), 5-6.
18. Van Henten, *The Maccabean Martyrs*, 119.

plays the part of the prime protagonist (προηγωνίζετο) and Antiochus struggles against him (ἀντηγωνίζετο). The seven sons also contended (ἠγωνίζοντο) for the prize of virtue. If the Maccabean martyrs remained virtuous, they would be crowned with victory, even in death. Here we see two essential motifs associated with the noble death—virtue and victory. Josephus likewise employs athletic imagery in speaking of the Essenes who 'triumphed over agonies' (τὰς μὲν ἀλγηδόνας νικῶντες) (*Ant.* 2.151). Here again, we see the motif of victory in death.

b. *Spectators Marvel at the Courage of the Martyrs*

If martyrdom may be compared to an athletic contest, it also has spectators.[19] 2 Maccabees tells us that the king and his men were 'struck with admiration' at the noble spirit of one of the martyrs (7.12). The writer tells us that the mother of the seven martyrs, a martyr herself, became an object of marvel (θαυμαστή) (7.20). The chief cause of the spectators' wonder is the martyrs' courage. The martyrdom of Razis is a public spectacle, during which Razis exhibited 'manly courage' by 'throwing himself into the crowd' (14.43). In *4 Maccabees*, the people explicitly play the role of the audience in the spectacle which is martyrdom (see *4 Macc.* 17.14). A martyrdom is, as Alois Stöger writes, an exhibition.[20] In this exhibition, martyrs inspire wonder in those who watch them die: 'By their courage and perseverance (ἀνδρείᾳ καὶ ὑπομονῇ) they won the admiration (θαυμασθέντες) not only of all mankind but even of their very torturers' (1.11). Eleazar, who endured torture like an athlete, 'won the admiration (ἐθαυμάζετο) even of his torturers' (6.11). The torturers especially marveled at his 'stoutness of heart' (εὐψυχία), which is a type of courage. Again, Eleazar, in death, was called 'most marvelous' (τὸ θαυμασιώτατον) (7.13). The tyrant himself expresses words of admiration for Eleazar (ὑμῶν θαυμάζω) (8.5). Again, we are told that the crowd marveled at the martyrs' courage (9.26). As recompense for their suffering, the martyrs were 'admired by mankind' (ὑπὸ τῶν ἀνθρώπων ἐθαυμάσθησαν) (18.3). So we see that spectators played an important role in the martyrdom, and that they admired the martyrs for their courage.

19. On this, see D. Potter, 'Martyrdom as Spectacle', in R. Scodel (ed.), *Theater and Society in the Classical World* (Ann Arbor: University of Michigan Press, 1993), 53-88.

20. Stöger, 'Eigenart und Botschaft der lukanischen Passiongeschichte', 8.

c. *Martyrs Die Willingly in Obedience to the Divine Will*

Of paramount importance to the martyrs is obedience to the divine will as found in Torah.[21] Particularly at issue are those portions of the divine law having to do with purity and holiness as defined in the Levitical codes. The challenge for the martyrs was to remain faithful to God and to their identity as Jewish persons. As van Henten puts it, the martyrs die not simply for the law, but for the 'Jewish way of life'.[22] Thus, in 2 Maccabees, Eleazar is 'ready to die rather than transgress the laws of our fathers' (7.2). *4 Maccabees* records how he refused to eat swine flesh, saying,

> We, Antiochus, who out of conviction lead our lives in accordance with the divine law (θείῳ νόμῳ), believe no constraint more compelling than our own willing obedience (εὐπειθείας) to the Law (νόμον); and therefore under no circumstance do we deem it right to transgress the Law (παρανομεῖν). (*4 Macc.* 5.16)

We see this emphasis on the Law also in the works of Josephus. The Essenes, we are told, refused to 'blaspheme the lawgiver or to eat some forbidden thing' (*War* 2.151). Likewise, Josephus praises the rabbis Judas and Matthias and their 40 disciples, who died 'on behalf of the ancestral law' (ὑπὲρ τοῦ πατρίου νόμου) (*War* 1.648-55). Josephus admires others for maintaining the ancestral ways:

> But those most esteemed, men of noble spirit, disregarded him, holding their ancestral customs (πατρίων ἐθῶν) to be more important than the punishment with which he threatened those who would not obey; for this reason...they were put to death. (*Ant.* 12.255)

In both the Maccabean literature and Josephus we see martyrs who have higher regard for ancestral and divine law than for their own safety.

d. *Martyrs Offer an Example for Others to Follow*

The Maccabean martyrs died in order to leave behind an example for others to follow.[23] In the words of van Henten, the martyrs become 'exemplary figures of the Jewish people'.[24] By dying courageously, Eleazar hoped to leave the young people 'a noble example (ὑπόδειγμα) of how to die happily (προθύμως) and nobly (γενναίως)' (2 Macc. 6.28).

21. For a thorough discussion of this, see van Henten, *The Maccabean Martyrs*, who links dying for the Law with dying for God (125-86).

22. Van Henten, *Maccabean Martyrs*, 188.

23. For a discussion of the mimetic value of the Maccabean martyrs' deaths, see Seeley, *The Noble Death*, 87-89.

24. See van Henten, *The Maccabean Martyrs*, 210-43.

The author tells us that Eleazar accomplished his goal: 'In this way he died, leaving in his death an example (ὑπόδειγμα) of nobility and memorial of virtue, not only to the young but also to the great majority of the nation' (2 Macc. 6.31). Likewise, in *4 Maccabees*, Eleazar's death serves as a paradigm for those who would follow him. He worries lest he become a 'pattern (τύπος) of impiety to the young, by setting an example (παράδειγμα) for eating of forbidden food' (*4 Macc.* 6.19). By his perseverance and good death, however, Eleazar becomes a good teacher (παιδευτής) (*4 Macc.* 9.6). Thus, the author of *4 Maccabees* credits him for showing good men how to die: 'You, father, by your perseverance in the public gaze, have made strong our adherence to the Law' (*4 Macc.* 7.9). So great is the story of the Maccabean martyrs, that Antiochus employed them as a pattern (ὑπόδειγμα) for his own soldiers to follow:

> For the tyrant Antiochus, taking as a model the courage of their virtue, and their constancy under torture, advertised their endurance as a pattern (ὑπόδειγμα) to his soldiers; he thus got them noble and courageous for infantry battle, and for siege; and he ravaged and vanquished all his enemies. (*4 Macc.* 17.23)

Even the martyrs' arch-enemy used them as an example of courage and virtue, values held by Jews and Greeks alike.

e. *Martyrs Expect Posthumous Honor*

The Maccabean martyrs offer last words by which they demonstrate and explain their peculiar cheerfulness. Their final statements combine two general characteristics. First, the martyr speaks defiantly to his executor, showing no deference to political authorities. Secondly, the martyr expresses a sure hope that he will be vindicated by God in the afterlife. In 2 Maccabees, the first son professes hope of vindication, even in the face of death: 'The Lord God is watching, and in very truth will have compassion on us' (2 Macc. 7.6). The second son combines defiance and belief in divine vindication in his dying words to Antiochus: 'You accursed wretch, you may release us from our present existence, but the King of the Universe will raise us up to everlasting life because we have died for His Laws' (7.9). Again, the fourth son dies with the 'hopeful expectation' of being 'raised up again', as opposed to Antiochus, who, he defiantly declares, will know 'no resurrection to life' (7.14). The sixth son likewise speaks defiantly: 'You will see how His [God's] overwhelming power will torment you and your offspring' (7.17). The seventh son, too, expects divine vindication in the afterlife: 'Indeed, our brothers, after enduring brief trouble, are under God's covenant for everlasting life' (7.36).

This knowledge of divine vindication enables the seventh son once again to speak boldly.

The expectation of divine vindication motivates the martyrs in *4 Maccabees*. Upon facing death the seven brothers speak in unison: 'Why, tyrant, do you delay?' (*4 Macc.* 9.1). They fully expect that they will be vindicated and that Antiochus will be punished:

> We, by our suffering and endurance, shall obtain the prize of virtue; and we shall be with God, on whose account we suffer; but you, for our foul murder, will endure at the hand of divine justice the condign punishment of eternal torment by fire. (*4 Macc.* 9.8-9)

As in 2 Maccabees, the martyrs address Antiochus directly and forcefully. The eldest brother calls Antiochus a 'foul tyrant, enemy of heaven's justice, savage of heart' (*4 Macc.* 9.15). The fifth brother addresses Antiochus as an 'enemy of virtue and enemy of mankind' (11.4). The seventh brother, when given the opportunity to speak to the king, begins, 'Sacrilegious man, tyrant most impious of all that are wicked' (12.11). He speaks defiantly, expressing his belief in divine vindication: 'In recompense for this, justice will keep you in store for intense and eternal fire and torment; and these shall never release you throughout time' (12.12).

Josephus similarly tells us that the Essenes, upon death, were 'mildly deriding of their tormentors' (κατειρωνευόμενοι τῶν τὰς βασάνους) (*War* 2.153). The Essenes spoke boldly, because they believed in divine vindication and the immortality of the soul (see *War* 2.154). As such, they were 'confident' that 'having resigned their souls', they would 'receive them back again' (*War* 2.153).

As we have seen in both Josephus and the Maccabean literature, the martyrs face death with a certain courage, which is grounded in the knowledge of divine vindication and manifests itself in bold speech.

f. *Martyrdom and 'Macabre' Death: The Detailed Description*

Within the Maccabean literature, the gruesomeness of the martyrs' death is recounted in excruciating detail so as to highlight their courage. Thus, we are told that Eleazar's family was 'tortured with whips and scorpions' (2 Macc. 7.1). The spokesman of the brothers was scalped and had his tongue and extremities cut off. Then, while still breathing, he was placed in a hot pan to fry to death (7.5). The other brothers likewise were tortured.

4 Maccabees goes further in describing martyrdom's gory details. The author informs us not only that Eleazar was whipped and beaten, but that 'his flesh was torn by the scourges; he was flowing with blood, and his sides were lacerated' (*4 Macc.* 6.6). Then, we are told, not only was he burned to death, but also his torturers 'burned him with evilly devised instruments, and flung him under the fire; and into his nostrils they poured a noisome brew' (6.25). It was only on being consumed 'to his very skeleton' that Eleazar offered a final prayer and died (6.26). The writer of *4 Maccabees* catalogues the instruments of torture used upon Eleazar's sons:

> The guards brought forward wheels and instruments for dislocating joints, racks and wooden horses, and catapults, and caldrons and braziers and thumbscrews and iron grips and wedges and bellows; and the tyrant then resumed, and said, 'Lads, be afraid'. (*4 Macc.* 8.13-14)

The modern reader is struck at the macabre depiction of the martyrs' death.[25] However, such details undeniably focus the reader on the extent to which the martyrs' courage was tested.

This type of macabre description of the martyr's death may also be found in Josephus. He records that Jews who rejected Antiochus' royal decree proscribing circumcision were tortured, whipped (μαστιγούμενοι), mutilated (λυμαινόμενοι), and then crucified (ἀνεσταυροῦντο) (*Ant.* 12.255). Afterwards, their wives were strangled, and their children were strangled and then suspended from the necks of their crucified parents (*Ant.* 12.256).[26] Elsewhere, Josephus writes approvingly of the Essenes who were 'racked and twisted, burnt and broken, and made to pass through every instrument of torture' (*War* 2.152). As in the Maccabean literature, Josephus describes the details of the martyrs' death to accentuate their nobility and heroism.

g. *Martyrdom in Josephus and Maccabees: A Summary*

The themes of Jewish martyrdom, as we have seen, overlap considerably with the features of a praiseworthy death, evidenced in the rhetorical tradition and the death of Socrates. All three traditions emphasize courage in the face of death and a willingness to die. As

25. For a discussion of 'Pathetic' history, see Hadas, *The Third and Fourth Books of Maccabees*, 99. Concerning the intensity of description, Hadas asks the modern reader to consider the Maccabean account in historical perspective: 'If his colors are anywhere too intense for modern readers, it is in the detailed description of the tortures. But here we have to do with a change of taste. Not only the roughly contemporary tragedies of Seneca and the epic of Lucan, but early Christian literature and even Elizabethan tragedy are (to use a word derived from) no less macabre' (102-103).

26. For a discussion of this incident, see Sam K. Williams, *Jesus' Death as Saving Event: The Background and Origin of a Concept* (Missoula, MT: Scholars Press, 1975), 75-76.

such, the martyrs triumph in their deaths, even as they remain obedient to the law.

Jewish martyrdom, to be sure, has its own accents and emphases. Especially in the Maccabean literature, we find an added emphasis on death as a public spectacle, in which the martyrs are depicted as athletes engaged in a contest against the forces of evil. This accent on spectacle manifests itself in a dramatic retelling of the act of dying itself. The Maccabean literature shows how the martyr dies and what he says upon his death. In this way, as van Henten writes, the martyr's life and death become a 'shining example for other Jews'.[27]

How do the rhetorical, Socratic, and martyrological deaths fit together? The rhetoric of death, as evidenced in Aristotle and the Athenian funeral speeches, begins primarily in a martial context. People are praised primarily for their valor and virtue in defense of country. This noble death tradition takes on a slightly different form in Socrates, the prime exemplar of the philosopher who dies not only for his country, but for the truth and integrity of his philosophy. Finally, the martyrological death, it would seem, should not be understood as a separate and distinct phenomenon, but as a combination of the rhetorical/military death and the Socratic/philosophical death to which is added the final component of allegiance to God and to the divine law. It is hard, for instance, to look at the story of the Maccabean martyrs, especially Eleazar, and not see motifs taken from the Socrates story. Both Socrates and Eleazar are older men who stand up for their moral convictions in the face of obdurate opponents, and both end up giving their lives for what they hold true. Likewise, the prominent Greco-Roman virtues in the Maccabean literature may be traced back to the Hellenistic values prescribed by Aristotle and Theon, and as evidenced in the funeral speeches and the *Lives* of Plutarch.

In summary, it appears as if the rhetorical presentation of the praiseworthy death was foundational in the ancients' understanding of noble death. The story of Socrates represents a development of that tradition in which the philosopher dies nobly for the sake of his philosophy. The Hellenistic–Jewish martyrdoms show that the tradition of the noble death was alive and well at the time of Luke. Evidently, Josephus, and even more so the writers of the Maccabean literature, appropriated many of the virtues associated with the praiseworthy death, and applied them for own their own purposes and their own audiences.

27. Van Henten, *The Maccabean Martyrs*, 295.

5

Luke's Presentation of Jesus' Death as Praiseworthy: An Appraisal of Sources

1. *Peculiarities of the Lukan Passion*

The Lukan passion narrative differs significantly from those of Matthew and Mark in both content and order. Some scholars have accounted for these differences by arguing that Luke was making use of different sources.[1] More recently, these differences have attracted the attention of those who see Luke's redactive hand at work. Scholars have come to appreciate Luke as an author and theologian who did not simply record established traditions, but shaped them for calculated effect.[2] Each evangelist demonstrates a distinct theological outlook. Luke, by a number of redactional changes, portrays Jesus as an innocent and virtuous man who faces death with courage and nobility. On the other hand, Luke omits a number of incidents found in the accounts of Matthew and Mark, including the following:

1. the description of Jesus as 'greatly distressed and troubled' upon entering the Garden of Gethsemane (Mk 14.33-34; Mt. 26.37);
2. Jesus' cry of anguish: 'My soul is sorrowful unto death' (Mk 14.34; Mt. 26.38);
3. the fact that Jesus 'threw himself to the ground' for prayer in the garden (Mk 14.35; Mt. 26.39);

1. See, e.g., Vincent Taylor, *The Passion Narrative of St. Luke: A Critical and Historical Examination* (SNTSMS, 19; Cambridge: Cambridge University Press, 1972).

2. For a discussion of the benefit of redaction criticism in understanding the passion narrative, see Neyrey's *The Passion according to Luke*, 1-3; see also Brown, *Death of the Messiah*, I, esp. 68-75, and also Frank J. Matera, *Passion Narratives and Gospel Theologies* (New York: Paulist Press, 1986), 152-55.

4. the statement that the crowd laid hands on Jesus prior to the disciple striking with the sword (Mk 14.46; Mt. 26.50);
5. the statement that Jesus was silent before Pilate (Mk 15.3-6; Mt. 27.14);
6. the mocking of Jesus by Roman soldiers (Mk 15.16-20a; Mt. 27.27-31);
7. the deriding of Jesus by passers-by (Mk 15.29; Mt. 27.39);
8. the unqualified statement that 'those who were crucified with him also reviled him' (Mk 15.32b; Mt. 27.44);
9. Jesus' cry that he has been forsaken by God (Mk 15.34; Mt. 27.46).

These omissions tend to remove much of the shame normally associated with crucifixion. Words and incidents which indicate Jesus' unwillingness to die on the cross are excised. Signs of fear or distress in Jesus are likewise absent. As a result, Jesus appears less a victim, and more in control of the circumstances. Furthermore, Luke removes some references to the public taunting of Jesus, and in doing so lessens the public shame of his death.

Likewise, Luke's passion narrative includes certain features, not found in the Matthean//Markan accounts:

1. the saying about the two swords (Lk. 22.35-38);
2. the note that Jesus went to the garden to pray 'according to custom' (22.39);
3. the fact that Jesus knelt, rather than threw himself to the ground, for prayer (22.41);
4. the fact that the disciples fell asleep due to grief (23.45);
5. the fact that Jesus confronted Judas with his treachery (22.48);
6. the fact that Jesus healed the slave's ear (22.51);
7. the fact that Jesus turned and looked at Peter, just as the rooster crowed, thus reminding Peter of his prediction concerning the three-fold denial (22.6);
8. the weeping and wailing of the women, and Jesus' address to them (23.27);
9. Pilate's three-fold declaration of Jesus' innocence (23.4, 14-15, 22);
10. the fact that Herod acknowledges Jesus' innocence (23.15);
11. the fact that a crowd of people is said to have been watching the crucifixion (23.35, 48);
12. the fact that one of the criminals crucified with Jesus was promised 'paradise today'(23.40-42);

13. the pious prayer of Jesus upon his death: 'Father, into your hands I commit my spirit' (23.46);
14. the declaration of the soldier that Jesus was truly 'righteous' (23.47);
15. the fact that upon Jesus' death, the crowds beat their breasts in sorrow (23.48);
16. the fact that Jesus is placed in a 'rock-hewn' tomb 'which had never been used' (23.53);
17. an additional reference to the women's preparation of spices and myrrh to anoint Jesus' body (23.56);
18. a great emphasis on the fact that Jesus' death is the fulfillment of prophecy (24.25-27, 44-46).

Raymond Brown, commenting on Luke's redactional work, notes that such changes are 'consonant with a Lucan christology that does not tolerate the human weaknesses allowed by the Marcan christology'.[3] Many, too, have noted that a number of the special Lukan features are apologetic in nature, as Luke aims to show that Jesus, and by implication his followers, are peaceful (innocent), honorable inhabitants of the Roman Empire.[4] Jesus' self-control and courage can also be seen in the way he handles himself in the garden and the arrest. Throughout the narrative, Jesus appears as the consummate example of piety. Accordingly, others see in the Lukan passion narrative a model for discipleship,[5] possibly even for martyrdom.[6]

This chapter has to do with Luke's tools and resources. What tools did Luke have at his disposal to shape his passion narrative? What literary models did he draw upon to depict Jesus' death as noble? Drawing upon the data of the previous chapters, I will ask in what measure Luke drew upon (1) the values of the noble death tradition embedded in ancient Greco-Roman rhetoric of praise, (2) the story of Socrates' death as recorded in the *Phaedo*, and passed down through the centuries, and (3) the tradition of Jewish martyrdom as seen in the Maccabean martyrs and the writings of Josephus.

3. Brown, *The Death of the Messiah*, I, 68.

4. See Cadbury, *The Making of Luke–Acts*, 305; Conzelmann, *The Theology of St. Luke*, 138-40.

5. See Brown, *The Death of the Messiah*, I, 75; Fitzmyer, *Luke*, I, 235-56; Matera, *Passion Narrative and Gospel Theologies*, 198-205.

6. See J. Ernst, *Das Evangelium nach Lukas* (Regensburg: Pustet, 1977), 643-44; M.J. Lagrange, *Evangile selon Saint Luc* (Paris: J. Gabalda, 1927), 593; Dibelius, *From Tradition to Gospel*, 201.

2. *A Review of Motifs, Found in Rhetoric, Socrates, and the Hellenistic–Jewish Martyrological Literature*

For the sake of convenience, I here include a review of the motifs found in the sources we have analyzed.

a. *The Praiseworthy Death, according to Rhetorical Convention*

According to the rhetorical guidelines evidenced in Aristotle, the Athenian funeral speeches, the Progymnasmata, and the *Lives* of Plutarch, a number of motifs are commonly employed in describing a death as praiseworthy. Noble deaths are characterized by the following characteristics: (1) virtue, especially courage and righteousness; (2) willingness to die; (3) being beneficial to others; (4) dying victoriously (not a victim); (5) being met in a timely manner, so that it is unique (i.e. a person acts first or alone); (6) posthumous honors.

b. *The Death of Socrates: Significant Motifs*

The primary motifs of the Socrates story include the following: (1) Socrates dies as a righteous man; (2) further, he is unjustly accused; (3) he willingly accepts his death as a necessity brought by the gods; (4) in obedience to the law he refuses to escape; (5) he maintains a cheerful courage; (6) he is surrounded by friends who grieve his death; (7) as a philosopher, he is trained for death.

c. *The Martyrological Motifs*

From what we have seen in the Maccabean literature and the works of Josephus, the martyrological literature bears witness to certain motifs, including the following: (1) martyrdom is a contest for virtue and victory; (2) spectators marvel at the courage of the martyrs; (3) martyrs die willingly in obedience to the law; (4) martyrs offer an example for others to follow; (5) martyrs expect posthumous honor; (6) the deaths of the martyrs are described in great detail.

3. *Luke's Presentation of Jesus' Death as Praiseworthy: Greco-Roman Rhetoric*

a. *The Courage of Jesus*

While righteousness is the chief of virtues, the one most frequently associated with a praiseworthy death is courage (ἀνδρία). According to Aristotle, courage 'makes men perform noble acts in the midst of dangers according to the dictates of the law and submission to it' (*Rhet.* 1.9.7). Elsewhere, Pseudo-Aristotle offers a fuller definition:

> To courage belongs to be undismayed by fears of death and confident in alarms and brave in face of dangers, and to prefer a fine death to base security, and to be a cause of victory. It also belongs to courage to labour and endure and play a manly part. Courage is accompanied by confidence and bravery and daring, and also by perseverance and endurance. (*Virt. Vit.* 4.4)

As such, courage is not reckless disregard for life, but the recognition and acceptance of one's duty (see Plutarch, *Pel.* 1.4). In battle, courage is often displayed in heroic acts of valor. In the face of trial and suffering, courage can manifest itself in other ways, such as obedience to the law, perseverance in adversity, and standing firm rather than fleeing danger. Aristotle tells us that a man is praiseworthy if he shows himself 'stout-hearted (μεγαλόψυχος) in adversity' (*Rhet.* 1.9.31). Plutarch praises Cratesicleia for being 'not one whit dismayed (ἐκπεπληγμένην) at death' (*Ag. Cleom.* 38.4). Courage also manifests itself in what the ancients term 'bold speech' (παρρησία). To the ancient Athenians, παρρησία, or speaking frankly, was the right of a free citizen of a democratic city-state.[7] To speak boldly was to avoid flattery. In Hellenistic times those who engaged in bold speech sought not to please, but to speak honestly, even in the face of danger.[8] As such, bold speech demonstrates courage in the face of power and peril.[9] Within the passion narrative, Luke portrays Jesus' courage in a number of ways, and in doing so, rhetorically heightens the praiseworthy quality of Jesus' death.

We see Jesus' courage in Luke's picture of him on the Mount of Olives. The portraits of Jesus in Matthew and Mark appear to run contrary to such a heroic ideal. Mark reports that as Jesus entered Gethsemane, 'he began to become greatly distressed (ἐκθαμβεῖσθαι) and troubled (ἀδημονεῖν)' (Mk 14.33). Further, we are told that as Jesus went to the Mount, he revealed a troubled inner state: 'My soul is sorrowful (περίλυπος) unto death' (Mk 14.34). Such a distressed, troubled, and sorrowful person does not exhibit the courage which

7. See Heinrich Schlier, 'παρρησία', in *TDNT*, V, 871-86.

8. See S.C. Winter, 'ΠΑΡΡΗΣΙΑ in Acts', in John T. Fitzgerald (ed.), *Friendship, Flattery, and Frankness of Speech: Studies in the New Testament World* (Leiden: E.J. Brill, 1996), 185-202.

9. Menander Rhetor in his *Treatise*, for instance, describes a certain governor's courage, especially his 'frankness' (παρρησία) in speaking to the emperor (2.416.23-24; see also 2.386.6-10). Likewise, one of the Maccabean martyrs displays his courage, through παρρησία (*4 Macc.* 10.5). For a discussion of bold speech, see J.T. Fitzgerald's *Cracks in an Earthen Vessel: An Examination of the Catalogues of Hardships in the Corinthian Correspondence* (SBLDS, 99; Atlanta: Scholars Press, 1988), 88-89.

characterizes a praiseworthy death. Plutarch, for instance, associates such emotions with weakness when he describes Philopoemen as 'overwhelmed with trouble and grief' (λύπῃ καὶ θορύβῳ) (*Phil.* 20.2). Accordingly, Luke omits these references, and by doing so removes vices associated with cowardice—the opposite of courage.

Luke especially highlights Jesus' courage by portraying him as one who engages in 'bold speech' (παρρησία). This bold speech, we have seen, is concomitant with courage. Jesus speaks boldly at his arrest, challenging the arresting party: 'Did you have to come with swords and clubs, as though I were an outlaw? I was with you in the temple every day, and you did not try to arrest me' (Lk. 22.52-53). Here he challenges the honor and rectitude of those who would arrest him,[10] while he himself remains the serene judge of what is taking place.[11] He contrasts his own courage, as one who speaks openly during the day, with the cowardice of his opponents, who have come to arrest him at night because they feared the crowds (see Lk. 20.19).

Jesus further employs bold speech in his appearance before the Sanhedrin. In a classic case of role reversal, the accused becomes the judge. The council challenges Jesus, 'If you are the Christ, tell us' (Lk. 22.67). The assembly hopes that Jesus will either renounce his messianic claim or be proven guilty of the charges brought against him. As Fitzmyer describes the situation, 'The first of the two questions put to Jesus is not idle; the interrogators are dead serious'.[12] Yet, Jesus, showing no fear, responds:

> If I tell you, you will not believe, and if I ask you, you will not answer. But from now on the Son of Man shall be seated at the right hand of the power of God. (Lk. 22.67-69)

Jesus' answer is, in the words of Tannehill, 'a bold affirmation', and evidence of Jesus' courage.[13] In fact, by claiming a seat near God, Jesus expresses two other themes found prominently in the noble death tradition, namely, victory and the expectation of posthumous honor. As Fitzmyer writes, Jesus asserts 'his victory over his adversaries—for he will be invested with the power of God'.[14] We shall see further examples of Jesus' courage in his willingness to die.

10. On this point, see John Nolland, *Luke* (3 vols.; Dallas: Word Books, 1993), III, 1089.
11. On Jesus' serenity, see Fitzmyer, *Luke*, II, 1449.
12. Fitzmyer, *Luke*, II, 1466.
13. Robert Tannehill, *Luke* (Nashville: Abingdon Press, 1996), 329.
14. Fitzmyer, *Luke*, II, 1463.

b. *Willingness to Die, in Accordance with Divine Will*

According to the values embedded in ancient rhetoric, a praiseworthy death is characterized by a willingness to die. The praiseworthy man chooses death over dishonor. Pericles praises the Athenian soldiers, for instance, because they *chose* (ἐβουλήθησαν) to fight and die (*History* 2.42.4). If Jesus had faced death unwillingly, he would have appeared cowardly. For this reason, Celsus chided Origen concerning Jesus' seeming unwillingness to die:

> Why does he mourn and lament and pray to escape the fear of death, expressing himself in terms like these: 'Father, if it be possible, let this cup pass from me'. (*Cels.* 2.24)

Luke appears sensitive to these types of charges, and shaped his passion narrative accordingly. In a number of places, Luke made redactional changes to depict Jesus' death as a willing choice.

For Luke, who wants to portray Jesus' death as praiseworthy, the story of Jesus in the garden as recorded by Matthew and Mark, would have been particularly embarrassing. In Mk 14.34-36, Jesus appears especially reluctant to die:

> And he [Jesus] said unto them, 'My soul is exceedingly sorrowful (περι-'λυπος) unto death. Stay here and watch.' He went a little farther, and fell on the ground, and prayed, that if it were possible, the hour might pass from him'. And he said 'Abba, Father, all things are possible for you. Take this cup away from me; nevertheless, not what I will, but what you [will].'

The Markan Jesus appears overwhelmed by grief, saying 'My soul is exceedingly sorrowful (περίλυπος) unto death (θανάτου)' (14.34). At the time, grief was deemed to be a vice, resulting from a lack of courage.[15] Even more, such grief would seem to indicate Jesus' unwillingness to die. According to the Markan account, Jesus then 'fell (ἔπιπτεν) onto the ground' (14.35). Desperate and overwhelmed by grief, Jesus appears out of control. Though he engages in prayer, Jesus strongly wishes to avoid suffering. In fact, having prayed once, Jesus 'prayed the same thing' (14.39), and afterwards, prayed a third time (14.41). This three-fold repetition suggests great reluctance on Jesus' part to follow the divine will.

As Jerome Neyrey has demonstrated, Luke redacted the garden scene in such a way as to remove these potentially embarrassing features.[16] These changes, Neyrey argues, are made to portray Jesus

15. See Diogenes Laertius, 7.110-12; Philo, *Leg.* 2.113. For a discussion of the ancients' view of grief, see Neyrey, *The Passion according to Luke*, 50-53.

16. See Neyrey, *The Passion according to Luke*, 49-68. See also his 'The Absence of Jesus' Emotions—Lukan Redaction of Lk. 22, 39-46', *Bib* 61 (1980), 53-171.

in a way which conforms more closely to 'popular philosophical attitudes of the day'.[17] That is, Luke depicts Jesus as virtuous and courageous.

What changes does Luke make? For one thing, the petition that the hour might pass is omitted (Mk 14.35). The Lukan Jesus willingly faces death. This willingness is also expressed in Jesus' prayer posture. Unlike, for instance, the desperate leper who 'fell on his face' before petitioning Jesus (Lk. 5.12), Jesus displays no desperation, and is not overwhelmed by the tension of the moment. In fact, he prays 'according to his custom' (22.39). Accordingly, instead of falling to the ground in prostration, the Lukan Jesus kneels in composed self-control (22.41).[18] Jesus' prayer posture is not dictated by his dire circumstances but by his customary piety. As John Kloppenborg comments on Jesus' kneeling posture, 'The effect is that Jesus prays, not in a state of collapse and desperation, but acknowledging the divine will, and obedient to it'.[19] We see this prayer posture again, not coincidentally, at the noble death of Stephen (Acts 7.60), who, like Jesus, bends his knees in the prayer of one willing to die.

Again, in the other Synoptics, Jesus prays three times to avoid the cup of suffering, a fact which accentuates Jesus' unwillingness to die. Yet, in Luke, Jesus prays only once. He no longer requests what is 'possible', but begins and ends his prayer with an obedient will: 'Father, if you will (βούλει), remove this cup from me; nevertheless not my will (θέλημα), but yours, be done' (Lk. 22.42).

The prayer's wording is significant; Luke's Jesus invokes the βουλή of his Father, a word linked closely to notions of divine necessity (δεῖ). Nowhere is this necessity clearer than in the matter of his death. For Jesus, three times we are told, it was necessary (δεῖ) for him to suffer, be rejected, put to death, and rise again (Lk. 9.22; 17.25; 22.7). This all must (δεῖ) take place in Jerusalem (13.33). Jesus must die, because God wills and plans it. As Fitzmyer notes, in Luke, the term βουλή refers to the 'fundamental divine "plan" for salvation which is realized in the activity of Jesus'.[20] The term also appears at decisive points in the book of Acts. On Pentecost, Peter interprets Jesus' crucifixion as part of God's βουλή (Acts 2.23), and later attributes the entire

17. Neyrey, *The Passion according to Luke*, 68.

18. Luke uses this same expression for kneeling (literally 'to lay down the knees') to describe the pious, dignified prayer offered by Stephen at his death (Acts 7.60; see also 20.36).

19. Kloppenborg, '"Exitus clari viri"', 112.

20. Fitzmyer, *Luke*, I, 179.

passion story to God's βουλή (4.28). Thus, when Jesus acknowledges the will of God, he willingly accepts his part in God's plan by willingly and courageously accepting his death. In addition to willingness, Jesus' prayer demonstrates his piety, and therefore righteousness before God.

The Angel and the Agony. When speaking about Jesus' willingness and courage to die, we must address the question of the Angel and the Agony (Lk. 22.43-44). There are two basic questions which these verses raise for this study: (1) Are these verses original to the text? (2) If the verses are authentic, how do they fit with Luke's attempt to depict Jesus' death as praiseworthy?

Admittedly, the textual evidence for vv. 43-44 is fairly equally divided.[21] This has led commentators to debate the issue of its inclusion on theological and literary grounds. Many have deemed the verses an interpolation because the ἀγωνία does not fit Luke's portrayal of an emotionally restrained Jesus. Streeter notes that it is particularly awkward for God's son to 'evince such a degree of *pathos*, and still more to require a created angel as a comforter'.[22] The picture of Jesus whose 'sweat became like drops of blood' is said to be particularly out of place.[23] Thus, Bart Ehrman and Mark Plunkett write, 'The critical theological issue concerns whether Luke sought to portray Jesus facing his death with fear and trembling or with cool equanimity'.[24] Ehrman and Plunkett are right to argue that Luke's portrayal of Jesus as one who exhibits self-control (σωφροσύνη) does not fit with the picture of a man who is overcome by emotion. Much, however, depends on whether ἀγωνία is understood as emotional distress or as a victorious struggle over the passions and Satan's temptations. We

21. The following manuscripts and ancient versions omit these verses: P69 (apparently), P75, ℵ (first corrector), A, B, N, R, T, W, 579, 0171*, f13; they are also omitted by Marcion, Clement of Alexandria, Origen, Athanasius, Ambrose, Cyril, and John Damascene. The following Greek manuscripts and ancient versions include these verses: ℵ*, D, K, L, X, Γ, Δ, Θ, Ψ; they are also read by Justin Martyr, Irenaeus, Hippolytus, Eusebius, Didymus, and Jerome.

22. B.H. Streeter, *The Four Gospels: A Study of Origins* (London: Macmillan, 1927), 137.

23. See Steven F. Plymale, *The Prayer Texts of Luke* (New York: Peter Lang, 1991), 61.

24. Bart Ehrman and Mark Plunkett, 'The Angel and the Agony: The Textual Problem of Luke 22.43-44', *CBQ* 45 (1983), 401-16 (411). Accordingly, Fitzmyer, while acknowledging that one cannot be apodictic on the matter, also omits the verses in his translation, noting, 'They add emotional details to what is otherwise a sober abridgment of the Marcan text' (*Luke*, II, 1444).

should note that Liddell and Scott define ἀγωνία first as 'a contest, a struggle for victory', second as a 'gymnastic exercise, wrestling', and only thirdly as 'agony, anguish'.[25] Commenting on this passage, Stauffer writes:

> It is in this sense that ἀγωνία must be understood in Lk. 22.44: γενόμενος ἐν ἀγωνίᾳ ἐκτενέστερον προσηύχετο. This is not as fear of death, but concern for victory in the face of the approaching decisive battle on which the fate of the world depends.[26]

Thus, we need not assume that ἀγωνία implies fear or lack of courage. Rather, it seems often to refer to 'supreme concentration of powers in the face of imminent decisions or disasters'.[27] Such a definition of ἀγωνία fits more closely with other New Testament usages of its cognates ἀγών and ἀγωνίζομαι. Paul often speaks of the Christian life in terms of an athletic struggle. This is well illustrated in 2 Tim. 4.7 where Paul, coming to the end of his own life, claims that he has 'fought the noble fight' (τὸν καλὸν ἀγῶνα ἠγώνισμαι).[28] Philo likewise describes a wise and virtuous man as one who conquers the emotions which normally accompany death as engaging 'in a contest of athletes' (ἐν ἄθλων ἀγῶνι) (*Prob.* 21).

In this light, it is worth noting that Luke employs the cognate verb ἀγωνίζομαι in the pericope of the narrow door (Lk. 13.22-30), where Jesus exhorts, 'Strive (ἀγωνίζεσθε) to enter through the narrow door, for many, I tell you, will seek to enter, but will not be able'. Here the term connotes an effort for righteousness, in which the 'workers of unrighteousness' are the losers (13.27). Commenting on this, Stauffer writes, 'The struggle for the kingdom allows no indolence, indecision, or relaxation'.[29] The struggle through the narrow door is an arduous one, but it is not marked by fear and trembling. Nor, I contend, is Jesus' ἀγωνία in the garden.

How precisely are we to understand this struggle? Jerome Neyrey argues persuasively that Jesus' ἀγωνία is a rematch of Jesus' struggle against the devil, a contest which began in the desert temptation/trial (Lk. 4.1-13).[30] This struggle has much to say about Jesus as the 'new Adam', who succeeds in overcoming temptation/trial (πειρασμός)

25. Henry George Liddell and Robert Scott, *Greek–English Lexicon* (Oxford: Clarendon Press, 1986), 10.

26. Karl L. Stauffer, 'ἀγών', in *TDNT*, I, 134-40 (140).

27. Stauffer, 'ἀγών'.

28. See also 1 Cor. 9.25, 27; Col. 1.29; 1 Thess. 2.2.

29. Stauffer, 'ἀγών', 137.

30. Neyrey, *The Passion according to Luke*, esp. 58-65.

where the first Adam failed.[31] Yet, it also shows Jesus as contestant in the struggle for virtue.[32] Will he remain a willing, courageous, and righteous man?

It is noteworthy that Jesus faces a 'trial' (πειρασμός) twice in Luke: once in the desert, and once in the garden. In the first πειρασμός, Jesus is engaged in a contest with the devil as his opponent, and overcomes the challenge. Luke tells us that after forty days Jesus was 'tempted' (πειραζόμενος) by the devil (Lk. 4.2). Jesus' final words to the devil are an admonition against temptation: 'You shall not overtempt (ἐκπειράσεις) the Lord your God' (4.12). Luke summarizes the temptation scene thus: 'And having finished every temptation (πειρασμόν), the devil went away from him for a time (ἄχρι καιροῦ)' (4.13). This was Jesus' first struggle in his contest with Satan, but it would not be his last.

Conzelmann claimed that the period between the desert temptation and the passion Jesus was 'free from Satan'.[33] Such an argument is overstated, for Jesus faces temptations and performs exorcisms throughout his ministry. Yet I would argue that Jesus' prayer in the garden marks the return of Satan to resume the conflict in full force. Although Satan is not specifically mentioned in the pericope, his role in the betrayal and death of Jesus is clear. Luke tells us that on that night 'Satan entered Judas' (Lk. 22.3). Further, we are told that Satan sought 'to sift Peter like wheat' (22.31). Surely, Jesus recognizes that he is fighting the forces of evil. After the betrayal, he says to his captors, 'This is your hour and the power of darkness' (22.53). Elsewhere Luke associates this darkness with Satan, who stands as enemy to the God of light (see Acts 26.18). Those who arrest Jesus become, as John Nolland writes, 'instruments of Satan against Jesus'.[34] As such, Jesus' prayer in the garden, bracketed by the *inclusio*, 'Pray that you do not enter into temptation (πειρασμός)', is best understood as the same type of contest as that which is described in the desert (Lk. 4.1-13). Jesus may be understood as engaged in a noble battle, the type which Greco-Roman auditors would understand as heroic and praiseworthy.

If we see the ἀγωνία as a struggle between Jesus and Satan, then we may better understand Luke's description of Jesus' physical state

31. Neyrey, *The Passion according to Luke*, esp. 172-79.

32. Elsewhere in the New Testament, 1 Tim. 4 employs such athletic imagery, urging: 'Train (γύμναζε) yourself in piety (εὐσέβειαν)'. Likewise, Paul compares himself to an athlete (ἀγωνιζόμενος) who submits to strict discipline in order to win the crown (1 Cor. 9.25).

33. Conzelmann, *The Theology of St. Luke*, 28.

34. Nolland, *Luke*, III, 1089.

in Lk. 22.44: 'his sweat became like drops of blood' (ὁ ἱδρὼς αὐτοῦ ὡσεὶ θρόμβοι αἵματος). There is some debate as to whether this verse refers to an actual bloody sweat,[35] or more likely, whether it is a metaphor for either the quantity of the sweat or the quality of the struggle. Some would argue that this vivid description does not fit in with Luke's description of Jesus as serene and confident.[36] However, such a criticism misses the point of Jesus' struggle. I think Sharon Ringe well captures the meaning of these verses when she writes:

> The word translated as Jesus' 'anguish', like the image of the sweat pouring off his body, comes from the realm of athletics. Both point not to the hesitancy or uncertainty, but to the intensely focused energy of an athlete just as the contest is about to begin.[37]

This athletic imagery includes themes commonly found in the noble death, including courage, virtue, and victory. In his seminal study on the matter, Neyrey calls Luke's description of blood-like sweat 'a vivid image of the struggle to be virtuous and faithful'.[38] Sweating drops like blood, Jesus is engaged in a noble contest.

Still, we must ask whether the appearance of the ministering angel fits in with Luke's presentation of Jesus as noble and praiseworthy according to the ancients' values. It has been argued that the angelic assistance portrays Jesus as weak and subordinate, which would make him ignoble.[39] The appearance of the angel, however, may be profitably viewed as a sign of God's favor. We should note that angels appear throughout Luke–Acts (Lk. 1.11-20, 26-38; 2.9-15; 24.23; Acts 5.19; 12.7-9; 15.10). These angels consistently appear as signs of divine benefaction and favor, and are instruments through which God offers deliverance and bestows honor. Notably, the strengthening angel is sent 'from heaven' (Lk. 22.43). As such, Jesus is strengthened and also honored by God. Commenting on this passage, Danker writes, 'The words "from heaven" accent the fact that God directs him [Jesus] on his present path'.[40] Even more, the angel serves as a portent of divine vindication. As Karl Rengstorf contends, the angel witnesses to the fact that though Jesus is rejected by the religious leaders, he remains

35. See A. Loisy, *L'évangile selon Luc* (Paris: E. Nourry, 1924; repr., Frankfurt: Minerva, 1971), 575.

36. See Robert Stein, *Luke* (Nashville: Broadman Press, 1992), 559.

37. Sharon Ringe, *Luke* (Louisville, KY: Westminster/John Knox Press, 1995), 266.

38. Neyrey, *The Passion according to Luke*, 64.

39. Certainly, other New Testament authors honor Jesus by stressing his superiority over the angels (see Col. 1.18; Heb. 1.4-7).

40. Frederick Danker, *Jesus and the New Age*, 355.

God's messiah.[41] As such, I contend that the angelic aid only serves to enhance the honor and praiseworthy status of Jesus, who is beloved of God.

Additionally, we note that Matthew and Mark both speak of ministering angels in the desert (Mt. 4.11; Mk 1.13). Luke, however, transfers the angelic aid to the garden trial, thereby linking the two events and heightening the drama of the passion. As Schulyer Brown writes, Luke's transfer of the angel from the desert to the garden supports 'his emphasis on the passion as the supreme trial of Jesus in his struggle against Satan'.[42] Again, Jesus is engaged in a contest for virtue, which is part and parcel of the praiseworthy death. In this contest, Jesus displays his courage and willingness to die.

Luke further underscores Jesus' willingness to die in his portrayal of the crucifixion. In both the Matthean and Markan versions, Jesus cries out that he has been forsaken by God (Mt. 27.46; Mk 15.34). His cry repeats the words of Psalm 22. Jerome Neyrey argues that Jesus' cry, echoing as it does a Psalm of Complaint, belongs to the category of socially sanctioned speech, and would have been understood as an honorable plea to God/Patron for vindication and the removal of his shame.[43] An observant Jew may have recognized that Jesus was praying a traditional prayer of the pious, and as such, expected that God would ultimately vindicate him. Still, to the Greco-Roman world, this connection would not have been so clear, and on the surface may have proved embarrassing. Such a cry could lead the reader to assume that Jesus was speaking impiously concerning God. Tellingly, Luke omits these last words of Jesus, and substitutes a prayer of submission to the divine will: 'Father, into your hands I commit my spirit' (Lk. 23.46). This prayer, taken from Ps. 31.5, underscores Jesus' piety and righteousness. It also underscores his belief that God would take care of him in the afterlife. As Brown writes, Jesus' prayer demonstrates that he dies 'without apprehension'.[44] Here we do well to note that Luke puts similar words into the mouth of Stephen, who prays, 'Lord Jesus, receive my spirit' (Acts 7.59). Thus, Jesus' pious willingness becomes an example for his followers.

41. Karl Rengstorf, *Das Evangelium nach Lukas* (Göttingen: Vandenhoeck & Ruprecht, 1962), 251.

42. Schuyler Brown, *Apostasy and Perseverance in the Theology of Luke* (AnBib, 36; Rome: Pontifical Biblical Institute, 1969), 8.

43. Neyrey, *Honor and Shame in the Gospel of Matthew*, 153-61.

44. Brown, *Death of the Messiah*, II, 1067.

c. *Jesus the Righteous One (δίκαιος)*

The ancients regarded righteousness (δικαιοσύνη) as the chief and highest virtue and as an essential component of the praiseworthy death. In this light, the soldier's acclamation at the death of Jesus is most striking: 'Truly this was a righteous (δίκαιος) man' (Lk. 23.47).

Before we consider the term δίκαιος according to its place in the noble death tradition, we should recognize that it may have a number of different—though not mutually exclusive—meanings. In short, Luke employs the term both theologically and apologetically. Many have noted that the term 'righteous' (δίκαιος) plays a significant role in Lukan theology, and that it functions as a christological title. Brian Beck argues that Luke depicts Jesus as the fulfillment of the Old Testament prophetic model of the suffering servant/prophet.[45] In the book of Acts, Peter, Stephen, and Ananias refer to Jesus as 'the Just One' (τὸν δίκαιον) (Acts 3.14; 7.52; 22.14), a title which recognizes Jesus as the fulfillment of Old Testament prophecy. Raymond Brown sees the title in Davidic terms with the result that Jesus is the long-awaited Just Messiah (see Jer. 23.5; Zech. 9.9; *Pss. Sol.* 17.32).[46] Still others, such as Dennis Sylva and Frank Matera have argued that the centurion's confession points to the fact that God is working his saving justice in the person of Jesus.[47] Finally, some argue that Luke, dependent on his sources, is remarking only on Jesus' steadfastness in death.[48]

G.D. Kilpatrick was among the first scholars to translate the term δίκαιος as 'innocent'.[49] Many others, recognizing Luke's own apologetic interests, have followed Kilpatrick's lead.[50] Such a translation takes into consideration the fact that the confession comes from the mouth of a Roman centurion, and further witnesses to the injustice of the crucifixion. Conzelmann argued that Luke wanted to demonstrate that Christianity need not be feared by secular authority. Far

45. See also D.L. Bock, *Proclamation from Prophecy and Pattern: Lucan Old Testament Christology* (JSNTSup, 12; Sheffield: JSOT Press, 1987), 143-48; Robert Karris, *Luke: Artist and Theologian: Luke's Passion Account as Literature* (New York: Paulist Press, 1985), 95.

46. Brown, *Death of the Messiah*, II, 1165.

47. See Frank Matera, 'The Death of Jesus according to Luke: A Question of Sources', *CBQ* 47 (1985), 469-85 (481-84); Dennis D. Sylva, 'The Temple Curtain and Jesus' Death in the Gospel of Luke', *JBL* 105 (1986), 239-50.

48. See Nolland, *Luke*, III, 1159.

49. G.D. Kilpatrick, 'A Theme of the Lucan Passion Story and Luke xxiii. 47', *JTS* 43 (1942), 34-36.

50. See, for instance, Fitzmyer, *Luke*, II, 1512; W.J. Harrington, *The Gospel according to St. Luke* (London: Geoffrey Chapman, 1968), 268.

from being an outlaw religion, Christianity required 'loyalty to the state'.[51] Thus Jesus is repeatedly declared innocent: by Pilate (Lk. 23.4, 14, 22), Herod (23.15), the penitent thief (23.41), and Joseph of Arimathea (23.51). To the chief priests and people, Pilate reported that he has found 'nothing blameworthy' (οὐδὲν εὑρίσκω αἴτιον) (23.4). Using the same language, Pilate told the chief priests and rulers that he was not able to find anything 'blameworthy' (αἴτιον) in Jesus (23.14). Luke tells us that a 'third time' Pilate declared that he had found nothing in Jesus worthy of death (αἴτιον θανάτου εὗρον ἐν αὐτῷ) (23.47). These declarations serve the apologetic purpose of demonstrating that Christians are law-abiding. It may further be argued that the declarations of Jesus' innocence are means by which Luke portrays Jesus' death as noble. Aristotle himself writes, 'It is noble to die before doing anything which deserves death' (*Rhet.* 3.11.8). Thus, Jesus dies innocently, and therefore nobly.

The centurion's declaration of Jesus' righteousness takes on even more meaning when it is considered in light of the noble death tradition. To call Jesus δίκαιος implies not only the absence of guilt, but the presence of virtue. According to Aristotle, praise is essentially 'the language which sets forth the greatness of virtue' (*Rhet.* 1.9.33). At the head of the virtues stands righteousness. By labeling Jesus as 'δίκαιος', Luke presents Jesus as one who is virtuous and praiseworthy. The soldier stands witness to one who has died nobly. As I will argue later, this reference may also have led the reader of Luke's Gospel to make comparisons between Jesus and Socrates, the prototypical righteous man.

According to Menander Rhetor (*Treatise* 1.361.22-25), being 'god-loved' (θεοφιλότης) and 'god-loving' (φιλοθεότεης) are both aspects of righteousness. By his loyalty to God and willingness to die, Jesus demonstrates his 'love' for God. In his pious prayers on the Mount of Olives (Lk. 22.46) and from the cross, Jesus addresses God as 'Father', thus embodying filial piety (Lk. 23.46). As Danker writes of Jesus' death prayer, 'Faithful and pious to the end, Jesus grants total power of attorney as he entrusts his "spirit" (*pneuma*) to that same Parent for safe keeping'.[52] In filial piety, Jesus follows the will of his father, giving evidence of trust and loyalty to his heavenly patron.

We also see that Jesus as a righteous man is 'God-loved' (θεοφιλότης). In the baptism and transfiguration, God declares Jesus to be his own son with whom he is well pleased (Lk. 3.22; 9.35). Jesus

51. Conzelmann, *The Theology of St. Luke*, 140.
52. Danker, *Jesus and the New Age*, 210.

himself attests to his God-loved status, declaring, 'The Spirit of the Lord is upon me' (Lk. 4.18). Peter speaks of Jesus as the one 'attested to by God with mighty works and wonders and signs which God did through him' (Acts 2.22). Jesus heals because 'God anointed [him] with the Holy Ghost and with power' (Acts 10.38; see Lk. 4.16-19). Thus, God declares Jesus his son, and confers his Spirit. In doing so, he bestows honor upon Jesus, and demonstrates his essential righteousness.

In Jesus' death, God once more declares fidelity to his son through divine portents and signs. In doing so, Danker writes, 'Luke rather follows the pattern set by ancient writers concerning people of exceptional merit'.[53] In Plutarch's *Lives*, as we have seen, Lycurgus is declared 'beloved of the gods' (θεοφιλεστάτῳ) when his tomb is struck by lightning (*Lyc*. 31.3). Romulus's praiseworthy death is accompanied by a solar eclipse (*Rom*. 27.6). So also Luke tells us that Jesus' death was accompanied by portents and signs. At Jesus' death, three portents take place: (1) darkness comes over the land (Lk. 23.44); (2) the sun stops shining (23.45); (3) the temple's curtain is torn in two (23.45). On one level, Luke interprets the darkness as an eschatological sign for the day of the Lord (see Lk. 2.17-21; Joel 3.1-5). However, Greco-Roman auditors would have also understood these portents as signs of divine judgment. For a parallel, we recall Plutarch, who tells us that the 'obscuration of the sun's rays' was a sign that 'the murder of Caesar was not pleasing to the gods' (*Caes*. 69.5).

d. *Jesus is not a Victim*

For a death to be praiseworthy, the one dying must be seen to have control of the situation rather than becoming a helpless victim of circumstances. According to Aristotle, a courageous man should not allow himself to be beaten (ἡττᾶσθαι), for victory (νίκη) is noble (*Rhet*. 1.9.25).

Luke portrays Jesus as master of his own destiny in a number of ways. First, he sets Jerusalem as his goal (Lk. 9.51), and predicted that he would be betrayed (22.21), denied (22.34), spat upon, mocked, insulted, and put to death (9.22, 44; 18.31-33). Jesus knew his fate and actively embraced it. A victim is governed by circumstances, but Jesus repeatedly knew and chose what would happen next. He understood that his suffering was a necessary step toward glory: 'Was it not necessary that the Messiah should suffer many things and enter into his glory (δόξαν)?' (24.26; see also 18.33; 24.7).

53. Danker, *Jesus and the New Age*, 210.

There are a number of instances within the passion narrative where Luke underscores the fact that Jesus was not the victim of circumstances. Even in the betrayal, the Lukan Jesus remains in control. Indeed, he predicts it (Lk. 22.21), and pronounces a judgment upon the betrayer (Lk. 22.22). Luke then reworks the betrayal scene itself to show Jesus in charge of the situation. As Fitzmyer notes, 'When compared with the Marcan account, the Lucan story of the arrest depicts Jesus himself dominating the scene'.[54] In Matthew//Mark, it is Judas who takes control of the situation: he plans the betrayal (Mt. 26.48//Mk 14.44), and proceeds to carry it out by identifying Jesus, speaking to him, and kissing him (Mt. 26.49//Mk 14.45). After this, the arresting party 'laid hands on him and arrested him' (Mt. 26.50//Mk 14.46). All of this happens to a passive Jesus who says not a word. In contrast, Luke tells us that even as Judas approaches Jesus with the intention of kissing him, it is Jesus who takes control of the situation, asking, 'Judas, are you betraying the Son of Man with a kiss?' (Lk. 22.48). As such, Jesus takes from Judas the initiative and does not wait to be taken. In this way, Luke avoids picturing Jesus as 'passively silent'.[55] Far from being a victim, Jesus remains in control.

Just as Jesus speaks with authority to Judas, so also he speaks authoritatively to the band arresting him, saying:

> Did you come out, as it were against a robber, with swords and clubs? Day after day, when I was with you in the Temple area, you did not lay a hand on me. But now this is your hour, and the power of darkness. (Lk. 22.52-53)

Here again we have an example of Jesus' bold speech (παρρησία). The arresting party's cowardice stands in stark contrast with Jesus' courage. Jesus had spoken openly in the temple, not afraid of those who plotted against him, while 'the scribes and chief priests had previously 'sought to lay hands on him', but 'feared (ἐφοβόθησαν) the people' (Lk. 20.19; see also 20.6). Furthermore, Jesus ironically notes that clubs, swords, and a night-time seizure are the only options for the chief priests and elders who had been reduced to silence by his public teaching (20.26, 40). Jesus moreover attributes the arrest to the arrival of the 'hour of darkness'. As such, the religious leaders' plot is a matter of divine necessity, part of God's greater plan (24.7, 26).

The story of the mocking of the soldiers (Lk. 22.63-65) may have also been potentially embarrassing to Luke as he attempted to portray

54. Fitzmyer, *Luke*, II, 1447.
55. See Brown, *Death of the Messiah*, I, 258.

Jesus as honorable and praiseworthy. Matthew and Mark depict Jesus as a passive victim who is beaten, spat upon, and ridiculed (Mt. 26.67-68; Mk 14.65). In Luke also, Jesus is the recipient of a brutal beating by those 'in charge of him' (Lk. 22.63-65). As soldiers blindfold Jesus and strike him on the face, they mock him, saying, 'Prophesy! Who hit you?' (22.64). As John Nolland writes, 'There is no reaction from Jesus; in this scene he is cast simply as a victim'.[56] If Nolland is correct, then Luke would be portraying Jesus in a way the ancients would have understood as ignoble and dishonorable. I would argue, however, that Jesus' victimhood is only apparent and is undercut by the Lukan use of literary irony. Here again, we see Luke's editorial hand at work, bringing honor to the potentially shameful account.

Specifically, Luke has moved the story of the beating to a position directly after Jesus turns to look at Peter (22.61). This gaze causes Peter to weep bitterly over his three-fold denial (22.62). Luke's reader/hearer knows, therefore, that Jesus can truly see and that he is a prophet sent from God. Fitzmyer hits the mark when he writes, 'Once again he gives the impression of one who is in control of the scene; he tolerates what is happening to him, because he is aware that this forms part of the consequences of the Father's will'.[57] Jesus was indeed a prophet who had predicted that he would have to face the soldiers' taunts and beatings (18.32-33). Though physically blindfolded, the reader knows that Jesus had foreseen what would happen. Thus, Luke would have his readers know that though Jesus appears to be a victim, he is in fact in control of his destiny. Through his use of literary irony, Luke turns Jesus' supposed shame into honor. In the words of Marion Soards:

> Luke built into his narrative an unstated communication between himself and his readers. He created a two-story phenomenon wherein there exists a sharp contrast between appearance and reality. The readers are invited to participate with Luke in the higher level of the narrative.[58]

The reader understands that Jesus is no mere victim, but is actively fulfilling the divine will. His tormentors, by contrast, clearly do not know what they are doing. Fooled by Jesus' surface appearance, they fail to see him for who he really is. As Soards adds, 'The effect of

56. Nolland, *Luke*, III, 1099.

57. Fitzmyer, *Luke*, II, 1461.

58. Marion Soards, 'A Literary Analysis of the Origin and Purpose of Luke's Account of the Mockery of Jesus', in Richard (ed.), *New Views on Luke and Acts*, 86-93 (92).

Luke's narrative technique is that the apparent victim becomes the one in charge and the apparent authorities become the victims of their own ignorance'.[59] As such, even in his silence and seeming passivity, Jesus is accomplishing the goal for which he was sent and acting in a praiseworthy manner.

We might also add that Luke tells us nothing about whether Jesus said anything while he was being beaten (Lk. 22.63-65). If he had cried out in pain, he might have been thought weak, and therefore ignoble. As David Seeley has demonstrated, the noble death is often marked by one's ability to overcome physical vulnerability.[60] Yet through Jesus' implied silence, the reader may infer that he demonstrated perseverance (ὑπομένη), a virtue concomitant to courage.[61]

The trial account might also create the impression that Jesus was a victim of forces outside his control. However, Jesus takes the occasion to proclaim his ultimate victory. When challenged as to whether he is the Christ, Jesus offers the following riposte: 'If I tell you, you will surely not believe; and if I ask, you will surely not answer' (Lk. 22.68). Jesus engages in the type of bold speech (παρρησία) associated with courage. Indeed, he witnesses to his ultimate victory, claiming that he will be given 'a seat at the right hand of God' (22.69). As Marion Soards writes, 'Therefore, when one hears Jesus speaking in the Assembly meeting, one knows his words are neither nervous chatter nor hollow boasts'.[62] Jesus remains in command of the situation.

Even on the cross he remains unbowed and active. Taunted concerning his identity as the Messiah and his supposed inability to save (Lk. 23.35, 37, 39), Jesus displays his kingship and saving power. When one criminal asks for a place in his kingdom, Jesus offers him paradise (23.42-43). As such, Fitzmyer writes, this episode presents the 'salvific aspect' of the crucifixion and points to Jesus' 'regal status'.[63] He does have a kingdom, and he welcomes the thief into it. Finally Jesus' life is not taken from him as if he were being ignobly conquered. Instead, in his dying words he willingly offers up his spirit to his Father (23.46).[64]

59. Soards, 'A Literary Analysis', 92.

60. Seeley, *The Noble Death*, 109-10, 118-19.

61. See Friedrich Hauck, 'ὑπομένη', in *TDNT*, IV, 581-88.

62. Marion Soards, *The Passion according to Luke: The Special Material of Luke 22* (JSNTSup, 14; Sheffield: JSOT Press, 1995), 108.

63. Fitzmyer, *Luke*, II, 1508.

64. His death is reminiscent of the Athenian soldier who 'in spirit remains unconquered by his opponents' (Demosthenes, *Funeral Speech* 19).

e. *Jesus Displays Customary/Habitual Piety*

Aristotle tells us that a man is to be praised 'if he has often been successful in the same thing', so that the deed may rightly be attributed to 'the man himself' and not 'a result of chance' (*Rhet.* 1.9.38). Aristotle understands that habitual actions reveal the true character of a man. A praiseworthy man is one whose training in piety has prepared him to face the most dire of situations in a manner consistent with his entire life of piety.

Luke draws upon this understanding of customary piety to depict Jesus' actions as honorable. As a boy, Jesus attended the Feast of Passover annually 'according to custom' (κατὰ τὸ ἔθος) (Lk. 2.41). Likewise, Jesus made prayer a customary part of his life, praying at significant junctures, such as at his baptism (3.21), the calling of the twelve (6.12), the first passion prediction (9.18), and the transfiguration (9.28). In 5.16, we learn that Jesus makes a practice of 'withdrawing into lonely places to pray'. In 6.12, we see Jesus praying 'on a mountain' and 'spending the whole night in prayer'. In 9.28, we are told that Jesus 'went up to the mountain to pray'. Finally, when Jesus enters Jerusalem, we are told that 'each evening he went out to spend the night on the mount, called Olivet' (21.37). From the evidence, we see that Jesus often withdraws to pray at night, on mountains and other lonely places. Therefore, it is totally in character that Jesus went out at night to (1) to pray (2) on the mountain (3) 'according to his custom' (κατὰ τὸ ἔθος) (22.39).

The prayer of Jesus in the garden, as demonstrated above, is not the plea of a desperate man. Instead, he prays according to his habitual piety (κατὰ τὸ ἔθος) (22.34), which has been the pattern and practice of his entire life. This habitual piety is yet another example of Jesus' righteousness. Commentators rightly note that 22.39 recalls 21.37, where Luke tells the reader that Jesus spent his final nights on the Mount of Olives. This serves the literary function of explaining how it was that Judas knew where to lead the arresting party.[65] As such, it adds to our picture of Jesus as a courageous man with nothing to hide. The phrase 'according to custom', Danker notes, 'suggests to Luke's public that despite his knowledge of the plot against him Jesus did not hesitate to meet his assigned responsibility'.[66]

65. See Fitzmyer, *Luke*, II, 1358, 1441.

66. Danker, *Jesus and the New Age*, 354. For other examples of customary piety, see Lk. 1.19; 2.42.

f. *Jesus, the Benefactor: He Acts for the Sake of Others*
According to Aristotle (*Rhet.* 1.9.16-24) and Theon (Prog. 9.29), especially noble are those deeds which are done for the sake of others, apart from selfish motives. Frederick Danker argued that Luke portrays Jesus as the 'Supreme Benefactor' who offers the gifts of God to his people.[67] Thus, employing the language of benefaction, Peter refers to Jesus as the one who 'went about doing good' (ὃς διῆλθεν εὐεργετῶν) (Acts 10.38).

Bruce Malina has refined Danker's thesis, describing the role of Jesus according to patron–client relationships. In the ancient world, the Patron–client relationship served as a type of dyadic contract of mutual support between individuals of unequal social standing. In this relationship, there would take place an exchange of goods. The patron, typically wealthy and well connected, would offer favors, such as political and physical protection as well as other goods difficult to obtain. In exchange, the client offered the patron his praise and loyalty, thereby increasing the Patron's prestige. The ancients commonly thought of the relationship between God and humanity in this way. According to Malina, Jesus performs the role of 'broker', between God, who is patron, and persons who are God's clients.[68] The broker, as the term implies, would act as a type of middle man between the patron and the client. As Broker, Jesus supplies to people the gifts of the heavenly Father (Patron).[69] As Broker, Jesus is called a 'savior' (Lk. 2.11; Acts 5.31; 13.23), who offers 'salvation' (Lk. 6.9; 7.50; 8.36, 48, 50; 9.56; 17.19; 18.42; 19.9; Acts 2.1, 40, 47, etc.). Luke sees Jesus' healing as part of his identity as Savior/benefactor (Lk. 6.9; 8.36, 48, 50; 18.42). He is specifically sent by God to offer services otherwise unattainable (Lk. 4.18-19). Jesus' beneficent healing was offered freely to many (4.40-41; 6.19; 7.12-17; 9.6; 14.1-6; 17.12-19). He becomes for the people a provider in the feeding of the five thousand (9.10-17). Thus, throughout his ministry Jesus serves as God's Broker.

Throughout his passion narrative, Luke continues to depict Jesus as God's broker and the people's benefactor, who performs deeds of healing, and provides for the salvation of others. This is first seen in the supper, in which Jesus offers bread as his body 'given *for you*' (ὑπὲρ ὑμῶν) and his blood 'shed *for you*' (ὑπὲρ ὑμῶν) (Lk. 22.19-20).

67. Danker, *Jesus and the New Age*, esp. 2-10.

68. Malina, *The New Testament World*, 101-103. Jesus is in fact called a 'broker' (μεσίτης) in 1 Tim. 2.5 and Heb. 7.25.

69. Bruce Malina, 'Patron and Client: The Analogy behind Synoptic Theology', *Foundation and Facets Forum* 4.1 (1988), 2-32.

This double emphasis upon both the body and blood being given for the sake of others is not found in Matthew and Mark, who tell us that the blood is shed 'for many', but remain silent concerning the body. Luke, with his double emphasis on the words 'for you', would have us know that Jesus' death is not simply a courageous act of personal piety, but it confers benefits to others. As Fitzmyer writes, 'The "for others" aspect of this added phrase is unmistakable...it implies the soteriological aspect of his life and death'.[70] When the Lukan Jesus speaks of his body and blood being given 'for you', he employs the language of benefaction associated with a praiseworthy death, as we saw in Greco-Roman rhetoric.

This interpretation is solidified by Jesus' words following the supper, in which he speaks specifically concerning Gentile benefactors and his own benefaction. First, he speaks of the misuse of benefaction: 'The kings of the Gentiles lord it over them and those in authority over them are addressed as "Benefactors" (εὐεργέται)' (Lk. 22.25). Clearly, the Lukan Jesus is not criticizing the use of the term itself, for Luke specifically tells us that Jesus himself served as a benefactor (εὐεργετῶν) (Acts 10.38). What Jesus criticizes is the type of benefaction which is self-serving, rather than for the sake of others.

Luke also demonstrates that Jesus is acting for the sake of others by presenting him as a healer in the passion narrative. Again, while each Synoptic tells the story of the cutting off of the servant's ear (Mt. 26.51; Mk 14.47; Lk. 22.50), only Luke narrates that Jesus healed the man (22.51). As Danker writes, 'Greco-Roman auditors would be impressed by Jesus' composure under pressure and by his persistent quality of beneficence'.[71] In death he confers benefits, even to his enemies.[72]

Luke alone among the evangelists records Jesus' final act of beneficence: the gift of salvation to the thief on the cross. Indeed, the theme of salvation underlies the entire crucifixion scene. The rulers mock Jesus, saying that he 'saved others' (ἄλλους ἔσωσεν) and challenging him to 'save himself' (σωσάτω ἑαυτόν) (Lk. 23.35). The soldiers likewise challenge Jesus, sneering that if he were the King of the Jews, he should 'save himself' (σῶσον σεαυτόν) (23.37). Similarly, the first criminal challenges Jesus' power as Messiah, saying, 'Are you really the Christ? Then save yourself and us' (σῶσον σεαυτόν καὶ ἡμᾶς) (23.39). Irony underlies these taunts, for the reader knows that Jesus

70. Fitzmyer, *Luke*, II, 1401.
71. Danker, *Jesus and the New Age*, 357.
72. Thus, Jesus models the behavior he asks of others (see Lk. 6.27-28).

is surely the Savior. As evidence of Jesus' role as Savior, Luke tells the story of the thief on the cross. One of the criminals asks, 'Jesus, remember me when you come into your kingdom' (23.42). Jesus answers, 'I tell you the truth, today you will be with me in paradise' (23.43). He who has been taunted for his supposed inability to save others does indeed save the thief. Such salvation is yet another example of Jesus as Benefactor. In all of this, Jesus shows himself to be a praiseworthy man who confers benefits to others.

g. *The Uniqueness of Jesus' Accomplishments*

According to Aristotle, the rhetor should amplify a person's praise by noting whether he did something 'alone, or first', or if he is 'chiefly responsible for it' (*Rhet.* 1.9.38). Likewise, Theon instructs his students that praiseworthy actions are those which 'occur in a timely manner, if one acted alone, or first' (*Prog.* 9.35-36).

Throughout Luke–Acts, the evangelist depicts Jesus and his work as unique. As Neyrey notes, Jesus is the 'foundational figure' in God's plan of salvation.[73] Prophecies, angelic visitors, portents and a special birth all mark Jesus as unique. In his baptism he is singled out. In his transfiguration, he stands 'alone' as God's son (Lk. 9.36). However, Luke does not explicitly label Jesus as 'unique' within the passion narrative. His singularity is rhetorically emphasized later. Peter declares that salvation can be found under 'no other name' (Acts 4.12). Similarly, Paul calls Jesus the 'first (πρῶτος) to rise from the dead' (Acts 26.23). This type of language is not found in the passion narrative.

h. *Public Grief*

While excessive grief is considered a sign of weakness in the one who is dying, the mourning of friends and admirers is an appropriate sign of honor for the one dying. We recall again Solon's wish, as recorded by Plutarch: 'May not an unlamented death be mine, but unto friends let me be a cause, when dead, for sorrow and sighing' (*Comp. Sol. Publ.* 1.4).

The first mention of grief on behalf of Jesus is found in the prayer in the Garden, where we are told that the disciples had fallen asleep, exhausted from grief (λύπη) (Lk. 22.45). Neyrey has argued that the disciples' grief is a sign of their weakness, the opposite of manly courage.[74] Grief (λύπη) has negative connotations in both Stoic

73. Neyrey, *The Passion according to Luke*, esp. 160-63.
74. Neyrey, *The Passion according to Luke*, 65-67.

philosophy and Hellenistic Judaism. In summary, Neyrey notes that λύπη might be: (1) one of the four cardinal passions (the opposite of a virtue and thus to be avoided), (2) a typical punishment for sin, and (3) an indication of guilt.[75] Accordingly, the disciples become, in effect, 'victims' of grief. Furthermore, the disciples' grief serves to accentuate Jesus' own temperance and courage.

We should also note, however, that the rhetoricians prescribe grief as the appropriate response to the suffering of a praiseworthy man.[76] I suggest that the ancients would not have understood the disciples' grief as a vice or passion, but as the means by which good people give honor to a praiseworthy man. Had the disciples been unmoved by their Lord's death, they would have reinforced the notion that his death was insignificant.

Concerning the grief which accompanied Jesus' death, Luke tells us that as he made his way to the place of the crucifixion, 'A large crowd of people followed Jesus, including women who mourned and lamented over him' (Lk. 23.27). Again, at Jesus' death, we are told that onlookers, 'beat their breasts' (23.48). These laments are echoed in Stephen's death, which was accompanied by a 'great mourning' (κοπετὸν μέγαν) (Acts 8.2). Such mourning is honorable and offers praise to the one who dies nobly.

Likewise, we may consider the mood of the people after Jesus' death. Instructive on this point is the Emmaus journey (Lk. 24.13-35). When Jesus appears to the two disciples, they are 'gloomy' (σκυθρωποί).[77] On one level, their sadness is due to their foolishness and slowness in understanding the necessity of Jesus' death and resurrection (24.25). On another, the disciples' grief is a sign of their affection for Jesus. His death does not go unlamented, and is, as such, honorable. Thus, Luke follows the noble death tradition in depicting Jesus' death as praiseworthy.

i. *Honorable Burial/Posthumous Honors*

As seen in the Athenian funeral speeches and the writings of Plutarch, an honorable funeral follows a praiseworthy life. Given Jesus' execution as a criminal, it would have been customary that his body

75. See Neyrey, 'Absence of Emotions', 157, and *The Passion according to Luke*, 65-68.

76. Luke also depicts Paul's bravery in the face of suffering (20.22), which is accompanied by the weeping of his friends (Acts 20.37). See Brown, *The Death of the Messiah*, 158.

77. On the gloomy mood of the disciples, see Nolland, *Luke*, III, 1208.

be left shamefully exposed on the cross, dishonorably deprived of burial rites, and consumed by animals.[78] Bodies were regularly left on the cross and became food for the crows (Horace, *Ep.* 1.16.48). Juvenal describes the manner in which a vulture took food from the crosses 'to bring some of the carrion to her offspring' (*Satires* 14.77). Pliny also reports that, in many cases, bodies were left hanging to be eaten by birds and scavenger animals (*Natural History* 36.107-108). Tacitus, writing during the time of Tiberius, reports, 'People sentenced to death forfeited their property and were forbidden burial' (*Annals* 6.29). Crucifixion thoroughly dishonored the bodies of the fallen.

However, as Fitzmyer says, Jesus receives 'an honorable and reverent burial'.[79] Luke describes Joseph as a man who was 'good and just' (ἀγαθὸς καὶ δίκαιος), who did not agree with the council's unjust condemnation. As a 'righteous' man, Joseph is able to recognize the essential righteousness of Jesus and provide an honorable burial. A parallel can be found in Acts, where we are told that 'Devout (εὐλαβεῖς) men buried Stephen' (Acts 8.2). In this way, Luke praises the fallen Christian martyr and offers the posthumous honor prescribed by the rhetoricians. Luke goes further in depicting a burial which the ancients would have recognized as noble. For instance, Joseph honors Jesus by wrapping Jesus' body in a 'linen cloth' (σινδόνι) (Lk. 23.53). First, we should note that Jesus' body was not left naked upon the cross, to become carrion for the birds (see *Satires* 14.77). The shameful nakedness of the cross is reversed by Joseph, who wrapped it up (ἐνετύλιξεν) (Lk. 23.53). Secondly, we should note that Joseph uses linen (σινδόνι) (23.53). G.W. Shea argues that Joseph's use of linen, a cloth of good quality, indicates Joseph's respect for Jesus.[80]

Usually, the bodies of the crucified were denied the honor of burial or else placed in a common pit fit for paupers. However, Luke tells us that Jesus was placed in an honorable tomb. Jesus' tomb was 'cut in rock' (Lk. 23.53). Such a tomb was no pauper's grave, and reflects Joseph's socio-economic standing.[81] As Robert Stein writes, 'Although he was crucified as a criminal, he was not buried as a criminal'.[82]

78. See Hengel, *Crucifixion*, esp. 143-46; Brown, *Death of the Messiah*, II, 1207.
79. Fitzmyer, *Luke*, II, 1524.
80. G.W. Shea, 'On the Burial of Jesus in Mark 15.42-47', *Faith & Reason* 17 (1991), 87-108 (98).
81. Nolland, *Luke*, III, 1165.
82. Stein, *Luke*, 600.

Luke further describes the tomb as one 'in which no one had yet been laid' (Lk. 23.53). This description echoes the portrayal of Jesus' regal entry into Jerusalem, on a colt 'on which no one has ever ridden' (19.30). As Fitzmyer writes, 'It is a detail that sets off the burial of Jesus from that of common criminals; it is a grave found worthy of Jesus, 'the King of the Jews'.[83] Donald Senior adds, 'As befitting his [Jesus'] dignity, the crucified body of the "King of the Jews" is laid in a tomb untouched by death'.[84] We also recall Plato's *Menexenus* where the orator praises the fallen, noting that, having been honored by the *polis*, they were the 'first to be buried in this tomb' (*Men.* 242C).

Likewise, the women play an important role in depicting Jesus' burial as praiseworthy. As we have seen, Plutarch highlights the nobility of Sulla's funeral by the fact that women contributed 'a vast quantity of spices' (*Sull.* 38.2).[85] So also Luke notes that Torah-observant women prepared 'ointments and spices' (ἀρώματα καὶ μύρα) for his body (Lk. 23.56). Again, we are told that the women carried their spices (ἀρώματα) to the tomb early the next morning (24.1). Such spices make for an honorable burial. We should note that this is not the first time ointment (μύρα) is used to honor Jesus. In the pericope of the Sinful Woman (7.36-50), she honors Jesus by pouring perfume stored in an alabaster jar on Jesus' feet (7.38). As Fitzmyer notes, 'She spares no lavishness'.[86] Such perfume, Jesus notes, is more valuable than oil, and is a sign of the honor given to him (7.46). So also, the costliness of the burial ointment adds to the honor given Jesus.

We should also note that Jesus' death was accompanied by the darkening of the sky and the renting of the temple veil. The darkness echoes Jesus' statement concerning 'the power of darkness' (Lk. 22.53), and Luke interprets it as an eschatological sign predicted by the prophet Joel (Acts 2.17-21). Likewise, the renting of the temple veil may symbolize any number of things, including God's wrath, the revealing of God's glory, and the end of the old covenant.[87] Luke, however, may have also intended these events to send another message to the Greco-Roman world at large. Raymond Brown writes:

83. See Fitzmyer, *Luke*, II, 1525, and Brown, *The Death of the Messiah*, 1255.

84. Donald Senior, *The Passion of Jesus in the Gospel of Luke* (Wilmington, DE: Michael Glazier, 1989), 151-52.

85. The fourth evangelist accentuates Jesus' honorable burial by reporting that Nicodemus brought some 100 pounds of spices (Jn 19.39).

86. Fitzmyer, *Luke*, I, 689.

87. See Nolland, *Luke*, III, 1157 for a list of possibilities.

> Luke showed interest in the universal effect of Jesus' birth in 2.1 by connecting it with the edict 'from Caesar Augustus that a census should be taken of the whole world', and he may be showing a parallel interest at Jesus' death.[88]

The Greco-Roman reader would have been educated to consider the darkness, eclipse, and torn veil in light of familiar parallels. As we have seen, divine portents and signs often accompanied the deaths of especially noble people. We recall Plutarch's Lycurgus, whose tomb was struck by lightning, proving that he was 'most holy and beloved of the gods (θεοφιλεστάτῳ)' (*Lyc.* 31.3). Again, at the death of Romulus, 'the light of the sun was eclipsed' (Plutarch, *Rom.* 27.6). Likewise, Caesar's murder was accompanied by the sun's darkening, by which the gods voiced their displeasure (Plutarch, *Caes.* 69.4-5). Plutarch, a rhetorically trained writer, records such phenomena as reactions of the heavenly world to earthly events. In Luke, the darkening of the sky and the renting of the temple veil occur contemporaneously with Jesus' final hours. The ancients would have been culturally conditioned to recognize these phenomena as signs of divine honor which accompany great men.

We may add God's greatest posthumous honor, namely, the raising of Jesus. The appearance at the grave of 'two men in clothes that gleamed like lightening' (ἀστραπτούσῃ) confirmed Jesus' status as one who has been raised by God (Lk. 24.4-8). In Acts, the apostles specifically preach that 'God raised him' (Acts 2.24; 4.10). Peter understands the resurrection as Christ's ultimate vindication, proclaiming, 'You killed the author of life, but God raised him from the dead' (Acts 4.15). Indeed, not only does God raise him, but grants him a title and position of honor: 'God made him Lord and Christ' (Acts 2.36). God furthermore 'glorified (ἐδόξασεν) him' (Acts 3.13). This is the language of praise and vindication. Jesus' supposed shame is turned into honor. In his death, burial, and resurrection, Jesus is depicted as honorable and praiseworthy.

j. *The Lukan Passion and the Rhetoric of Noble Death: A Summary*

We have seen that Greco-Roman authors employed rhetoric in the praise of those who died nobly. Luke portrays Jesus' death as noble and praiseworthy, according to the same standards. Far from being afraid, Jesus demonstrates courage as he steadfastly heads towards the cross. In righteousness, he willingly embraces the divine will. His prayers reflect the customary righteousness of a pious man. Not a

88. Brown, *Death of the Messiah*, II, 1043.

victim of circumstances, he remains unbowed in death. Fittingly, Jesus' death is met with honorable grief and posthumous honors. The only aspect of the praiseworthy death which is not explicitly depicted in the Lukan passion is its 'uniqueness'. However, his singularity is explicitly praised by Paul, who calls him the 'first (πρῶτος) to rise from the dead' (Acts 26.23). The following table displays the motifs of a noble death as they match with the Lukan Passion:

Table 3. *The Motifs of Noble Death and the Lukan Passion*

Motifs	*Rhetoric of Noble Death*	*Lukan Passion*
Virtue: courage	×	×
Virtue: righteousness	×	×
Willingness to Die	×	×
Benefits Others	×	×
Not a Victim	×	×
Unique	×	?
Public Grief	×	×
Posthumous Honors	×	×

We see from the chart above that the Lukan narrative makes use of well-known prescriptions for praising noble death. Luke surely had the literary resources, as well as the motive, for picturing Jesus as a man who would appear praiseworthy in the eyes of the Greco-Roman world. We are therefore led to believe that Luke was drawing upon the common tradition of the noble/praiseworthy death to write his passion narrative. This helps the reader understand Luke's motives, not simply in this or that pericope, but in the passion narrative as a whole.

4. *The Story of Socrates and the Lukan Passion*

a. *The Injustice of Jesus' Sentence*

Clearly, the theme of injustice runs through the Socrates story and the Lukan passion narrative. Socrates is accused by those who 'told many lies' (*Apol.* 1A), and is a victim of a 'false accusation' (*Apol.* 19B; 21B). The falsity of the charges is apparent, Socrates argues, for he has always 'taught openly' (*Apol.* 19D). Thus, it became proverbial that Socrates had died unjustly.[89] So also Luke is keen to demonstrate the injustice of the sentence against Jesus. Both Matthew (26.66) and Mark (14.64) record guilty verdicts against Jesus, but not Luke.

89. See Plutarch, *Phoc.* 38.2; *Mor.* 538A; Josephus, *Apion.* 2.263; Diogenes Laertius, *Socr.* 2.35.

Instead, as we have seen above, three times Pilate declares Jesus innocent (Lk. 23.4, 14, 22). The first charge, that he opposed paying taxes to Caesar, was patently false, as shown by Jesus' teaching in the temple: 'Give unto Caesar what belongs to Caesar' (20.25). The second charge, that he was 'inciting the people to revolt (23.5, 14), is shown to be false by Jesus' rebuking of the disciple who cut off the ear of the high priest's servant (22.51). The theme of unjust punishment culminates in the words of the thief on the cross, who says, 'We die justly (δικαίως), for we are getting what our deeds deserve. But this man has done nothing wrong (οὐδὲν ἄτοπον)' (23.41). Ancient readers may well have heard echoes of Socrates in Luke's account of an unjust trial.

b. *Jesus Dies as a Righteous Man*

Plato tells us that before Socrates drank the cup of poison, he piously offered a prayer to the gods for a fortunate departure from this life (*Phaedo* 117C). Plato ends his story of Socrates with these words of praise:

> Such was the end, Echecrates, of our friend, who was, as we may say, of all those of his time whom we have known, the best and wisest and most righteous. (*Phaedo* 118)

Thus, the final word in the famous story of the most noble death in all antiquity, is the testimony that Socrates was 'most righteous' (δικαιοτάτου). Xenophon also concludes his memoirs with a description of Socrates as righteous (δίκαιος) (*Mem*. 4.8.11). As such, 'righteousness' is especially associated with Socrates and the story of his death.

Likewise, the righteous death of Jesus culminates in the pious and righteous prayer with which he ends his life: 'Father, into your hands I commend my spirit' (Lk. 23.46). Following this prayer, his executioner declares, 'Surely, this was a righteous man' (ὄντως ὁ ἄνθρωπος οὗτος δίκαιος ἦν) (23.47). Given the enduring popularity of the Socrates story, as well as Luke's own knowledge of the Socratic tradition, it would be reasonable to see Luke's treatment as an echo of the Socrates story. This is not to deny that the term δίκαιος may not be working on other levels.[90] However, Luke's choice of this term, replacing the Matthean and Markan designations of Jesus as 'Son of God', would have pricked the ears of his Greco-Roman auditors, and led them to think of Jesus as a great teacher and righteous man in the tradition of Socrates

90. See Tannehill, *Luke*, 347.

c. *Jesus' Death as Necessity Brought by God*

As Socrates judged death a necessity (ἀνάγκην) sent by the gods (*Phaedo* 62C), Luke also emphasizes the divine necessity of Jesus' death.[91] In Luke, δεῖ indicates divine necessity, a theme which permeates his Gospel. As a boy of twelve, Jesus claims divine necessity (δεῖ) as his reason for remaining in the temple (Lk. 2.49). Likewise, his preaching ministry is a matter of divine necessity (δεῖ) (4.43). This necessity is nowhere more clear than in the matter of his death. Jesus understands that it is necessary (δεῖ) for him to suffer, be rejected, killed, and rise again (9.22; 17.25; 22.7). This must (δεῖ) happen in Jerusalem (13.33). For Jesus, as for Socrates, the divine will took precedence over his own, as evidenced by the Mount of Olives prayer (22.42). That Jesus' death is in accordance with the divine will is seen in Luke's depiction of Jesus' death as the necessary fulfillment of prophecy. Thus, it was 'necessary (δεῖ) that the Christ suffer these things and enter into glory' (24.25-27). Again, Jesus said, 'These are my words that I spoke to you while I was still with you, that it is necessary (δεῖ) that everything written about me in the law of Moses and prophets and the psalms must be fulfilled' (24.44). This theme of divine necessity would surely have echoed in the ears of those who remembered that Socrates, too, faced death as a divine necessity.

d. *Jesus Does Not Try to Escape, but Obeys the Law*

Socrates, though condemned unjustly, refused to escape, arguing, 'The law must be obeyed' (*Apol.* 19C). We see Jesus' obedience to the law in the betrayal-and-arrest scene (Lk. 22.47-53). Notably, one of the disciples brandished a sword, saying, 'Lord, shall we strike with the sword?' (22.49). Jesus had earlier quieted talk of violence (see 22.38).[92] Yet, in an instant, a disciple 'struck the slave of the high priest and cut off his right ear' (22.50). This provided Jesus an opportunity to escape. As Nolland assesses the situation, the disciples 'want to fight their way out of the situation'.[93] Rather than ward off arrest, Jesus submits to it. Taking command, Jesus rebuked his disciples, saying, 'No more of this' (22.51). Then Jesus rectified the situation by healing the servant's ear, a feature not found in Matthew or Mark.

91. The prominence of the term δεῖ in Luke is seen in contrast to its limited use in Mark (8.31) and Matthew (16.21). For a further discussion of divine necessity in Luke, see Fitzmyer, *Luke*, I, 179-81, and Walter Grundmann, 'δεῖ, δέον, ἐστί', in *TDNT*, II, 21-25.

92. Fitzmyer (*Luke*, II, 1448) notes that this question is found only in Luke, and links the arrest to the Two-Swords pericope.

93. Nolland, *Luke*, III, 1090.

Here, Jesus' actions are reminiscent of Socrates, who argued against requiting evil with evil: 'Then we ought neither to requite wrong with wrong nor to do evil to anyone, no matter what he may have done to us' (*Crito* 49C).

Jesus proceeds to offer a defense against the charge that he is an outlaw who would be expected to flee capture:

> Then Jesus said to the chief priests and captains of the temple and elders, who had come out against him, 'Have you come out as against a robber (ληστὴν), with swords and clubs. When I was with you day after day in the temple, you did not lay hands on me. But this is your hour, and the power of darkness. (Lk. 22.52-53)

The irony of Jesus' question is apparent, especially as he had earlier foretold the event in accordance with Scripture:

> For I tell you that this scripture must be fulfilled in me, 'And he was reckoned with among the lawless (ἀνόμων); for what is written about me has its fulfillment'. (Lk. 22.37)

Thus, Luke makes it clear that Jesus was law-abiding. However, I do not think the parallels are strong enough to suggest that Luke was drawing upon the Socrates story. Once imprisoned, Jesus does not have the opportunity to escape.

e. *Cheerfulness/Jesus is Not Overcome with Grief*

Socrates displayed a remarkable cheerfulness, even to the point of death. We are told that in the face of death, he did not weep, but gently took the cup of poison without changing the expression of his face (*Phaedo* 117B). As he raised the poison to his lips, 'he very cheerfully and quietly drained it' (*Phaedo* 117B). Plato would have us know that Socrates handled the cup gently and easily, without shaking or tremors of fear.

In this vein, Luke removes the description of Jesus being 'sorrowful unto death' (Mt. 26.38//Mk 23.34). Like Socrates, the Lukan Jesus displays a certain gentleness. This gentleness may be seen in the healing of the servant's ear (Lk. 22.51) and his word to the thief (23.43).

Finally, Luke records that as Jesus was dying, he 'called out with a loud voice (φωνήσας φωνῇ μεγάλῃ)' (Lk. 23.46). Luke's description is a gentler redaction of Matthew (27.46) and Mark (15.34), who tell us that Jesus cried out (ἀνεβόησεν/ἐβόησεν).[94] As such, Luke once again emphasizes Jesus' calm demeanor upon dying.

94. For further discussion of Jesus' death cry in Luke, see Brown, *The Death of the Messiah*, II, 1066-69.

f. *Jesus and the Question of Being 'Trained' for Death*
Is there anything in the Lukan Passion narrative which indicates that Jesus appears, like Socrates, as an athlete, 'trained' for death? We recall that Socrates compared himself to an athlete, and rhetorically asked whether he should listen either to the crowd (foolish public opinion), or to the trainer (παιδοτρίβης) (*Crito* 47B). According to Socrates, the wise man 'ought to fear the blame and welcome the praise of that one man [i.e. the trainer] and not of the multitude' (*Crito* 47B). As an example, Socrates offers the following:

> And he [the athlete] must act and exercise and eat and drink as the one man who is his director and who knows the business thinks best rather than as all others think. (*Crito* 47B)

The athlete (the wise man), acts, exercises, eats, and drinks as his trainer commands.

So also Jesus' time in the desert may be seen as a time for training, during which Jesus is tested as to whether he will follow the will of his trainer (God). Luke himself calls it a test or trial (πειρασμόν), in which Satan does the testing. Would Jesus eat bread offered by the devil, or listen to the word of his trainer (God, as he speaks in Scripture)? (Lk. 4.2). Along parallel lines, as he later prays in the garden, the question before him is whether he will drink the cup which his trainer has offered to him (22.42). As we have seen, Jesus' time on the Mount of Olives is depicted as an athletic contest (ἀγωνία). This athletic imagery is reinforced by the picture of Jesus sweating: 'His sweat became like drops of blood' (22.44). The trials throughout Jesus' ministry revolve around the question of whether he will listen to the crowds and seek power, or accept the suffering which God has chosen for him. These trials come to a climax on the Mount of Olives, where Jesus begins to face his final trial in earnest. The athletic imagery is reminiscent of Socrates' story. However, the Athenian sage's struggle is not depicted in such vivid physical terms.

We may also think of Jesus' prayer as preparation and training for death. As we have seen, at every major juncture in his life Jesus turns to prayer (see Lk. 3.21; 5.16; 6.21; 9.18, 28-29; 11.1; 22.32, 41). Jesus thereby serves as a model for Christians to follow. Moreover, Jesus' life of prayer is not only an example of his piety, but also of training for his death. He is able to face the agony in the garden because he has been training for such a time as this. When first we learn that the scribes and Pharisees became enraged at Jesus, and discussed among one another what to do with him, 'Jesus went up to a mountain to pray, and spent the whole night praying to God' (6.12). Again, during the final days, having entered into Jerusalem, 'he would go and spend the nights on the hill called the Mount of Olives' (21.38). By the exercise of prayer, Jesus prepares himself for death. Like Socrates, he follows the advice of his trainer and says, 'Thy will be done' (22.42).

We must ask, however, whether this is more than an example of similarity. To be sure, both Socrates and Jesus prepare themselves for death. Luke makes use of athletic imagery, but in a more subdued way. Furthermore, God is nowhere explicitly called a trainer. This makes Luke's dependence upon the story of Socrates less probable here.

g. *The Role of Friends and Condign Mourning*

One of the striking elements and appealing features of Socrates' death story is that up until the end the sage is surrounded by friends. The Lukan Passion likewise highlights the role which Jesus' friends/disciples played during his last days. Notably, Luke omits Jesus' prediction of the disciples' desertion (Mk 14.27-28) as well as the actual desertion (Mk 14.34), and has no account to parallel the flight of the naked young disciple (Mk 14.51-52). This suggests that Jesus is not abandoned or left alone by his followers. On the contrary, as Jesus dies, Luke, alone among the Synoptic writers, reports, 'All his acquaintances (οἱ γνωστοὶ αὐτῷ) stood at a distance, including the women who had followed him from Galilee and saw these events' (Lk. 23.49). This creates the impression that the disciples were present throughout.[95] Moreover, in the garden scene, the disciples appear to be, as Kloppenborg writes, 'genuine disciples rather than failures'.[96] The disciples' loyalty is demonstrated in their grief. In Matthew and Mark, Jesus' disciples fall asleep three times, due presumably to their 'weak flesh' (Mt. 26.41; Mk 14.38). This repeated sleep accents the disciples' weakness, and even disobedience. Luke, conversely, mentions the disciples' sleep only once, and attributes it to their grief (λύπης) (22.45). On one level, grief was understood by the ancients as a vice, a succumbing to one of the four cardinal passions, whose opposite virtue is courage.[97] However, the role of grief in the Socrates story is more nuanced, as we have seen above. Grief is a demonstration of loyalty, and accents the nobility of the one dying. As Kloppenborg observes, 'Grief is just as typical in those who attend dying

95. See Kloppenborg, '"Exitus clari viri"', 113.
96. Kloppenborg, '"Exitus clari viri"', 114.
97. See, for instance, Philo, *Leg.* 2.113; 3.250; for a discussion of the matter, see Neyrey, *The Passion according to Luke*, esp. 50-53, 65-67.

heroes as is its absence in the hero itself'.[98] Through their grief, the disciples give honor to Jesus. Whether this motif can be traced back directly to Socrates is less clear. As we have seen, mourning regularly accompanied the death of a noble person.

Having discussed the weeping of friends, there remains the matter of Xanthippe, Socrates' wife. Xanthippe plays the role of the grieving woman, 'wailing and beating her breast' (βοῶσάν τε καὶ κοπτομένην) (*Phaedo* 60B). Grieving family members do not play a significant role in the Lukan Passion account. Luke, uniquely among the evangelists, tells us that as Jesus made his way to the cross, women 'were striking themselves and mourning for him' (ἐκόπτοντο καὶ ἐθρήνουν) (Lk. 23.27). This grief, however, does not have a close parallel in the story of Socrates and seems more closely related to the grief associated with the noble death.

h. *The Prophecy of Retribution*

Socrates understood his prophecy as fitting a pattern: 'For I am now at the time when men most do prophesy, the time just before death' (*Apol.* 39C). Socrates predicted that those who condemned him would be punished (*Apol.* 39C). In particular, the philosopher prophesied that those who voted for his condemnation would ultimately be condemned by later generations:

> Those who will force you to give an account will be more numerous than heretofore; men whom I restrained, though you knew it not; and they will be harsher, inasmuch as they are younger, and you will be more annoyed. (*Apol.* 39D)

His accusers might silence the messenger, but the message would live on.

Are there parallel prophecies in Luke?[99] Certainly, Luke emphasized Jesus' prophetic role, especially in his final days (i.e. Lk. 22.12, 16, 18, 21-22, 34, 37).[100] Jesus' prophecy before the Sanhedrin merits closer attention. As we have seen, he here claims ultimate vindication: 'But from now on the Son of Man will be seated at the right hand of the power of God' (22.69). Jesus' prophecy, however, differs significantly from that of Socrates. As Fitzmyer writes, Jesus claims 'a

98. Kloppenborg, '"Exitus clari viri"', 114.

99. A pattern of prophesying before death can be seen elsewhere in Luke-Acts. Compare the activities of Simeon (Lk. 2.25-35); Anna (Lk. 2.36-38); and Stephen (Acts 7).

100. For discussion of Jesus as God's final prophet, see Matera, *Passion Narratives and Gospel Theologies*, 205-12.

heavenly status'.[101] The retribution will come from Jesus' own judgment rather than from his followers, as in the case of Socrates.

We may add that Jesus also speaks an extended prophecy of woe as he is being led out for crucifixion (23.27-31). To the mourning women, Jesus says, 'Daughters of Jerusalem, do not weep for me, but weep for yourselves and your children' (23.27). He foretells of the day when barrenness would be preferred to motherhood (23.29). Like Socrates, Jesus predicts that things will be worse for his fellow citizens when he is gone: 'If these things are done when the wood is green what will happen when it is dry?' (23.31).[102] The meaning of this prophetic judgment is by no means clear. As Nolland summarizes, 'The active agent(s) for this proverb has been variously taken as God, the Romans, the Jewish leaders, or the Jewish people more generally'.[103] However, it seems clear that Jesus is predicting disaster for the people of Jerusalem. In this, there is a parallel with Socrates, who predicted difficult times for his fellow Athenians (*Apol.* 39D). It would be tenuous, though, to claim that Luke is drawing from the Socrates story in this instance, though the reader may have heard a faint echo here also.[104]

i. *Jesus and Socrates: Evaluating the Parallels*

Certainly there are a number of striking parallels between the stories of Jesus and Socrates. We may ask whether these parallels, taken together, make a case for literary dependence or influence of some sort.

As a preliminary matter, I think that the evidence is clear that Luke, as an educated Hellenistic author, knew the story of Socrates, and could also have expected his reader to be familiar with it. As we have seen, Luke alluded to the Socrates' story in Acts (4.19; 5.29; 17.16-34). Not surprisingly, many of the possible Socratic motifs overlap with motifs in the noble death tradition. The refusal of the

101. Fitzmyer, *Luke*, II, 1462. See also Darrell L. Bock, *Blasphemy and Exaltation in Judaism: The Charge against Jesus in Mark 14.53-65* (Grand Rapids: Baker Book House, 1998), 206-207, 237.

102. The proverb presents an argument *a minore ad majus*. If the Romans treat the Jews poorly in good times, how much worse will it be in bad times? For loose parallels, see 1 Pet. 4.17, and *Seder Elijah Rabbah* 14: 'When the moist [sc. wood] catches fire, what will the dry do?' For further discussion see Neyrey, *The Passion according to Luke*, 114; Brown, *The Death of the Messiah*, II, 925-27.

103. Nolland, *Luke*, III, 1138. See also Fitzmyer, *Luke*, II, 1498; Stein, *Luke*, 586.

104. Luke may here be echoing Isa. 54.1, a beatitude which reads: 'Blessed are the barren'. See Fitzmyer, *Luke*, II, 1498.

noble person to escape, we have seen, was part of a much greater tradition which included, but was not encompassed by, the Socrates story.[105] Likewise, the fact that Jesus and Socrates did not grieve their own deaths can be attributed to a larger tradition of courage and fearlessness in the face of death.[106] The mourning of friends and bystanders, likewise, is a motif present throughout Plutarch's *Lives*, and is difficult to tie directly to Socrates' story. The prophecy of retribution is interesting, but the similarity is not close enough to warrant positing the Socrates story as a source.

Other parallels, though, are more persuasive. Jesus' innocence and unjust sentence echo the story of Socrates and are not motifs of the noble death tradition. Likewise, Jesus' death as a necessity from God resonates closely with the story of the Athenian sage, and is not a feature of the noble death. Further, I would contend that in labeling Jesus as 'righteous' Luke is making a conscious nod to the Socrates story. An educated person would have recognized Socrates' righteousness, if not from Plato or Xenophon, then from the chreiai which circulated widely (see Theon, *Prog.* 90-91).

The following table displays motifs found in the story of Socrates' death and the Lukan passion:

Table 4. *The Death of Socrates and the Lukan Passion*

Motifs	*Socrates*	*Lukan Passion*
Unjust Sentence	×	×
Dying as a Righteous Man	×	×
Death as Divine Necessity	×	×
Refusal to Escape	×	×
Not overcome with grief	×	×
'Trained' for death	×	×
Role of Friends/Condign Mourning	×	×
Prophecy of Retribution/Woe	×	o

105. We have seen, willingness to die nobly, rather than escape shamefully, is praised in the Athenian funeral speeches (i.e. Lysias [*Funeral Speech* 62], Demosthenes [*Funeral Speech* 37], etc.); as well as in Plutarch's *Lives* (i.e. *Pel.* 1.3; *Comp. Nic. Crass.* 5.2). This falls into line with the ancients' long-held ethical and rhetorical tradition, which promotes righteousness (δικαιοσύνη) and its duties to God and country, and courage (ἀνδρία), which frowns upon escape, which is deemed cowardly.

106. We have seen that courage was exhorted by Aristotle (*Rhet.* 1.9.29), and was praised in Athenian funeral speeches (i.e. Lysias [*Funeral Speech* 63], Demosthenes [*Funeral Speech* 19], Hyperides [*F.S.* 3]), as well as in Plutarch's *Lives* (i.e. *Caius Gracch.* 19.3, and *Phoc.* 36.1).

Some of the above parallels are stronger than others, as I have indicated. Thus, I think in this instance, the possible influence of the Socrates story or the noble death tradition is not an either/or question. Luke, I think generally draws upon the noble death tradition, but, at times, nods to Socrates' story. By alluding to the Socrates story, Luke subtly reminds his readers that good men indeed are punished unjustly, and that the cross's supposed shame should not prevent them from seeing Jesus' true honor.

5. *Martyrological Themes in Luke*

We now turn to Luke's possible use of Hellenistic–Jewish martyrological motifs in the shaping of his passion narrative. As with the case of Socrates, we shall see some overlapping of themes. Yet, by noting specific aspects of the martyrological deaths, we will better see whether Luke used that literature as a source, or whether Luke, like the Maccabean writers, drew upon earlier resources.

a. *Jesus' Death as Contest for Virtue and Victory*

Martyrological literature compares martyrdom to an athletic contest or spectacle. The Maccabean literature, in particular, may have influenced Jesus' agony (ἀγωνία) in the garden. In 2 Macc. 3.14, 16, and 15.19, the term ἀγωνία describes the struggle of the Jewish people during times of persecution. In *4 Macc.* 13.15, 16.16, and 17.11-16, the related term ἀγών more clearly depicts the martyrs' struggle as a contest between good and evil.

I have argued that Jesus' ἀγωνία was not the anguish of a weakened man, but the description of a heroic struggle between Jesus and Satan. As the Maccabean martyrs faced the temptations of Antiochus, so Luke portrays Jesus confronting Satan and the power of darkness (see Lk. 22.3, 31, 53). This ἀγωνία, which began during the desert trial (πειρασμός) (4.1-13), culminates in the garden trial (πειρασμός) (22.40, 46). To accentuate Jesus' trial in the garden, Luke reports that while he was in his ἀγωνία, 'his sweat was like drops of blood falling to the ground' (22.44). Hartmut Aschermann was among the first to see in the Lukan description of Jesus' blood and sweat a parallel to the martyrdoms of *4 Maccabees*.[107] The Maccabean martyrs are said 'to defend the Law with their own blood, and with their noble sweat (ἰσίῳ αἵματι καὶ γενναίῳ ἱδρῶτι) in the face of sufferings unto death' (*4 Macc.* 7.8). According to Aschermann, Luke's description of bloody sweat

107. Aschermann, 'Zum Agoniegebet Jesu'.

reveals his intention to depict Jesus as a martyr engaged in a prayer-struggle in the style of the Maccabean martyrologies.[108]

To accentuate further Luke's depiction of Jesus as a contestant in a martyrdom, he tells us that Jesus, being in the agony, 'prayed more earnestly' (ἐκτενέστερον προσηύχετο) (Lk. 22.44). This is reminiscent of Nicanor's noble death recorded in 2 Maccabees, who 'with all zeal (μετὰ πάσης ἐκτενίας) risked body and life in behalf of Judaism' (2 Macc. 14.38). This battle not only reveals Jesus as praiseworthy, but also as a contestant in a struggle against evil.

Martyrological literature portrays the martyrs' opponents as antagonists in a contest. Jesus' antagonists include Judas, the Jewish leaders, and perhaps, to a lesser degree, Pilate. However, in the Lukan Passion narrative the ultimate adversary is Satan (σατανᾶς, διάβολος). The devil, who had left Jesus in the desert 'until an opportune time' (ἄχρι καιροῦ) (Lk. 4.13), returns in the passion for the final contest. Jesus had forewarned of the time when the devil would come (ἔρχεται ὁ διάβολος), and the disciples would enter into a 'time of testing' (ἐν καιρῷ πειρασμοῦ) (8.12-13). Though he had been at work throughout Jesus' ministry, the devil intensified his attacks in the passion. As John Nolland writes, 'The passion period is such a time of special Satanic onslaught'.[109] Satan enters Judas (22.3) and spurs Peter's denial (22.31). Again, it is the power of darkness (ἡ ἐξουσία τοῦ σκότους) that is at work in Jesus' arrest (22.53). As Danker comments, 'Luke wants his public to know that the events which follow are to be seen in a cosmic dimension as a contest between demonic forces and God'.[110] Thus, we see parallels here between Jesus' struggle against the powers of darkness and the Maccabean martyrs' contest for virtue.

b. *People as Spectators*

In *4 Maccabees*, the people side neither with martyr athletes nor with their antagonists, but stand on the sideline, as spectators at a great contest (*4 Macc.* 17.14). *3 Maccabees* likewise speaks of people coming to the martyrdom as if to a spectacle: 'The crowds in the city assembled for the piteous spectacle' (*3 Macc.* 5.24). This martryological background may help explain the role which the people play in the Lukan passion. While the people in Mark take a hostile attitude

108. Aschermann, 'Zum Agoniegebt Jesu'. See also Holleran, *The Synoptic Gethsemane*, 92-101.

109. Nolland, *Luke*, III, 1031.

110. Danker, *Jesus and the New Age*, 342.

towards Jesus (see Mk 15.13, 15, 29), Luke portrays them as neutral spectators. Thus, we are told that 'the people stood watching' (εἱστήκει ὁ λαὸς θεωρῶν) (Lk. 23.35).[111] As Arthur Just describes the situation, 'The text gives the impression that they are struck silent at the spectacle before them'.[112] Having watched the crucifixion, the spectators become sympathetic: 'When all the people who had gathered to witness this spectacle (θεωρίαν) saw (θεωρήσαντες) what took place, they beat their breasts and went away' (23.48). This is the language of public spectacle. As Brown writes, '[T]heir observation led to repentance'.[113] In their mourning, the Lukan crowd is reminiscent of those who watched the Maccabean martyrs, and admired their perseverance (*4 Macc.* 17.13-14).[114] Thus, for Luke, Jesus' death is not simply a historical event, but may be a spectacle which serves as a witness to Jesus' status as God's martyr.

c. *Jesus' Obedience to the Divine Will*

An essential component of Hellenistic–Jewish martyrdom is the martyr's unswerving obedience to the divine and ancestral law. For his refusal to eat swine flesh, Eleazar is put to death (*4 Macc.* 5.16). Jesus also understands his death as a matter of divine necessity, recorded in the Law of Moses (Lk. 24.44). However, there does seem to be a major difference. Jesus does not offer up his life in defense of the Jewish way of life, nor is he tempted to break the ancestral laws by which the Jews defined themselves. Furthermore, his accusers include the Jewish leaders themselves (22.66). In this regard, Jesus stands in the tradition of Old Testament prophets who suffered at the hands of God's people.[115] Jesus dies not as a defender of ancestral law, but as a rejected prophet. As such, Luke does not appear to be influenced by the martyrological literature in this instance.

d. *Jesus' Dying as an Example for Others to Follow*

Eleazar, leading the Maccabean martyrs, died as an example (ὑπόδειγμα) for others to follow (2 Macc. 6.28). Likewise, Luke presents

111. This is most likely an allusion to Ps. 22.7. See J.H. Reumann, 'Psalm 22 at the Cross', *Interpretation* 28 (1974), 39-58.

112. Just, *Luke*, II, 935.

113. Brown, *Death of the Messiah*, III, 990. Luke also links the beating of the breast and repentance in the story of the tax collector and the Pharisee (Lk. 18.13).

114. See van Henten, *Maccabean Martyrs*, 121-22.

115. Charles Talbert distinguishes between martyrs who die at the hands of God's people and those who die at the hands of Gentiles, in 'Martyrdom in Luke–Acts', esp. 104-105.

Jesus as a model for discipleship.[116] As Jesus walks toward the cross, so also should his disciples daily take up theirs (Lk. 9.23; 14.27). As Jesus struggles on the Mount of Olives, his disciples will have to follow (ἠκολούθησαν) his example (Lk. 22.39). Thus, Jesus predicts his own fate as well as the fate of his disciples when he says:

> Before all these things take place, however, they will lay hands on you and persecute you, handing you over to the synagogues and prisons, leading you before kings and governors on account of my name. It will lead you to giving testimony (εἰς μαρτύριον). (21.12-13)[117]

Jerome Neyrey has demonstrated that this passage is programmatic for the book of Acts. He writes, 'For each item and each phrase in Jesus' prophecy is quite literally and amply fulfilled in Acts'.[118] Jesus was the first martyr, in whose footsteps his disciples would necessarily follow.

We can see this especially in the way that Luke describes Stephen's death (Acts 7.54–8.1), which is recounted in imitation of Jesus' death: (1) both appear before the Sanhedrin (Lk. 22.66-70; Acts 6.12); (2) both respond to the questioning of the high priest (Lk. 22.67, 70; Acts 7.1); (3) Jesus predicts, 'From now on, the Son of Man will be seated at the right hand of the mighty God', while Stephen cries out, 'I see the heavens open and the Son of Man standing at God's right hand'—thus both predict posthumous honor of divine vindication; again, (4) both offer up their spirits to God/Jesus in prayer (Lk. 23.46; Acts 7.59); (5) both men are falsely accused (see Lk. 23.2; Acts 6.1, 2).[119]

Further, we might add the fact that Stephen prayed for those who put him to death (Acts 7.60). In some Lukan manuscripts (i.e. א*, C, L, Γ, Δ), Jesus is recorded as having prayed a similar prayer: 'Father, forgive them; they do not realize what they are doing' (Lk. 23.34). Many manuscripts, though, omit the saying (i.e. P75, B, D*, W, Θ. 0124, 579, 1241). Most likely, a scribe, noting the above parallels between the deaths of Stephen and Jesus, inserted the saying to make the death scenes even more similar. If so, the scribe also understood the Lukan Jesus as a model for martyrs who would follow.

116. For a discussion of Jesus' passion as the model for discipleship, see Fitzmyer, *Luke*, I, 235-57; Matera, *Passion Narratives and Gospel Theologies*, 198-205; Tannehill, *The Narrative Unity of Luke–Acts*, 203-74.

117. For an extensive list of parallels between Jesus' passion, and the fate of his disciples in *Acts*, see Neyrey's *The Passion according to Luke*, 84-88.

118. Neyrey, *The Passion according to Luke*, 88.

119. For a good discussion of the parallels between Stephen and Jesus, see Talbert, 'Martyrdom in Luke–Acts', 100.

e. *Jesus' Expectation of Posthumous Honor*

Eleazar met death with pleasure (2 Macc. 6.28), and the Essenes maintained good cheer though in mortal danger (*War* 2.153). Their happiness was the product of their confidence in divine vindication, which included God's compassion in the afterlife (2 Macc. 7.36), as well as God's judgment upon their accusers/tormentors/judges (*4 Macc.* 12.12).[120]

To be sure, Jesus speaks confidently in the face of judgment, employing frank speech (παρρησία) (see Lk. 22.66-71). However, the Lukan picture of Jesus, compared to the picture of the Maccabean martyrs, is much more subdued. Absent from the Lukan picture is a description of Jesus facing death with anything that could be described as pleasure. Like the Maccabean martyrs, Jesus expresses faith in his own vindication, predicting that he will 'be seated at the right hand of the mighty God' (Lk. 22.69). However, Jesus offers no words of condemnation to those who carry out his execution. As Frank Matera notes, he 'dies with peaceful words'.[121] In this, Luke does not appear to follow the martyrological model.

f. *'Macabre Death' and the Lukan Passion*

The martyrological literature described the deaths of the Maccabean martyrs in ways we can only label 'macabre'. Their deaths are described in excruciating detail which adds to the spectacle of the martyrdom. This component is notably lacking in the Lukan Passion narrative. While Luke records the fact that the guards mocked and beat Jesus, he offers no details about the lashes or the skin's abrasions (Lk. 22.63). Likewise, Luke tells us none of the excruciating details of crucifixion. We are told simply, 'There they crucified him' (23.33). As Raymond Brown ironically remarks, 'Yet in all comparable literature, has so crucial a moment ever been phrased so briefly and uninformatively?'[122] As such, the tone of the Lukan passion narrative is quite different from the martyrological literature.

g. *Luke and Martyrdom: A Summary*

Clearly there are instances in which the Lukan passion shares motifs familiar to us from Hellenistic-Jewish martyrdom literature. The contest of martyrdom is hinted at in Jesus' garden ανωνὶα against

120. In the desire for vindication, the martyrs are reminiscent of Aristotle, who declared vengeance noble (*Rhet.* 1.9.24).

121. Matera, *Passion Narratives and Gospel Theologies*, 186.

122. Brown, *Death of the Messiah*, II, 945.

Satan (Lk. 22.39-46). Jesus' blood-like sweat finds its closest parallel in the Maccabean martyrs. As with the martyrs, Jesus' death is meant to serve as an example for others to follow. Luke's passion shares other motifs with the martyr literature. Like the martyrs, Jesus dies courageously and willingly, expecting posthumous honors. Likewise, the people who watch the crucifixion may be seen as spectators of the spectacle which is taking place in front of them (23.45, 48). Admittedly, this motif, in comparison with the tradition of the martyrs, is subdued in the Lukan passion. These are motifs which we have seen in the noble death tradition as well.

However, there are dissimilarities as well. The Lukan Jesus does not die on account of the ancestral law. Furthermore, we notice in him none of the defiant joy expressed by the Maccabean martyrs. Finally, Luke offers us none of the macabre details of Jesus' death. The following chart offers a visual summary of our findings:

Table 5. *Martyrdom and the Lukan Passion*

Motifs	*Martyrdom*	*Luke*
Virtue and Victory	×	×
People as Spectators	×	×
Obedience to Ancestral Law	×	o
Dying as an Example for Others	×	×
'Defiant' Expectation of Posthumous Honor	×	o
'Macabre' Death	×	o

We have to conclude that if Luke borrowed certain themes from the martryological tradition, he did not rely heavily upon it. More likely, both Luke and the martyrological tradition were recipients of a greater tradition of noble death. In any case, the death of Jesus surely served as a struggle, which was meant to demonstrate fidelity to God, and to encourage others to follow in the martyr's footsteps.

6. *Luke's Use of Sources: A Brief Summary*

As we have seen, Luke formed and fashioned his passion narrative in order to present Jesus as noble and therefore praiseworthy according to well-known standards of the Greco-Roman world. As such, his account does much to moderate the perceived shame of the cross, and to paint a portrait of Jesus as a man of honor and virtue. Luke makes it clear that though crucifixion may be shameful, Jesus does not fit the stereotype of the crucified man.

The single most effective tool or resource at Luke's disposal was the longstanding tradition of noble death, as embodied in Greco-Roman rhetoric and learned in the progymnasmata. As we have seen, the third evangelist made a number of changes at the redactional level which demonstrate his employment of the tradition. First, we consider the scene on the Mount of Olives. Luke omits references to Jesus as 'distressed or troubled' (Mk 14.33-34; Mt. 26.37), as well as his words of sorrow (Mk 14.34; Mt. 26.38). Further, the Lukan Jesus does not 'throw himself to the ground' as if he is overcome by the situation (Mk 14.34; Mt. 26.38). Instead, he faces death piously and willingly. He kneels for a prayer in which he consents to the divine will (Lk. 22.41-42). All these details may all be explained by Luke's consistent use of the noble death tradition.

We see, likewise, that the Lukan Jesus remains fully in control of the situation, and so is clearly not a victim of circumstances. In the arrest, Jesus is not passively betrayed, but takes charge of the situation, showing that he knew what Judas was doing (Lk. 22.48). Jesus remains law-observant, even as his disciples fight to save him. Far from being a law-breaker, Jesus is innocent of every charge (23.4, 14, 22).

Throughout the passion, furthermore, Jesus continues to act for the sake of others (see Lk. 22.51). His nobility is seen most clearly on the cross, where he acts on behalf of one of the criminals (23.43) and offers a pious prayer (23.46). Finally, his praiseworthy status is accented by his honorable burial, for which the women prepared spices (23.53, 56). All of these changes are consonant with Luke's desire to present Jesus as praiseworthy according to the ancients' own definitions. In death, he is courageous, righteous, and willing. He acts for the sake of others, and is accorded posthumous honors. All of these motifs help Luke make Jesus more appealing to his Greco-Roman audience.

The question of Luke's use of the story of Socrates' death and the Maccabean literature is more problematic. A number of motifs are commonly shared. For instance, all three traditions promote virtue and courage. Having said that, there are peculiarities of the Socrates story and the martyrological tradition that Luke appears to have drawn upon. Thus, when the centurion declares Jesus 'righteous', Luke appears to be drawing from the tradition of noble death. That is, he depicted Jesus as virtuous in death. Given Luke's education and his allusions to Socrates elsewhere, it seems likely that Luke was alluding to the sage in 23.47. Among the ancients, Socrates was the most prominent 'righteous man', and Luke was cognizant of this fact. Likewise, Jesus' prayer on the Mount of Olives includes themes drawn from noble death, especially in seeing death as a victorious struggle. The bloody sweat of Jesus is a motif more closely associated with martyrdom (22.44). Again, the theme of dying as an example for others to follow is especially prominent in the martyrological literature; however it can be found in the noble death tradition as well.

7. *Furthering Scholarship*

What, we may ask, has this study done to further Lukan scholarship? First, this work has identified specific basic resources which the ancients used in depicting a death as noble. Secondly, this work has argued that Luke has drawn upon these resources in mitigating the shame of the crucifixion. A number of features of the Lukan passion are illuminated when read against the template of the noble death tradition. Thirdly, this work further establishes Luke as a Hellenistic author of high rhetorical skill and social status. The changes which he makes in the passion narrative are small, but significant. Luke shows himself to be an author of considerable skill. Marion Soards puts it well when he writes, 'Luke was no mere provincial, but rather a cosmopolitan believer who styled his story from and for an appreciation for subtlety'.[123] As we have seen, the Lukan depiction of Jesus' death draws from a wide variety of sources. He has taken as part of his aim the portrayal of Jesus' death as praiseworthy, as indeed, Luke understood it to be. In doing so, he offered a model for Christians to emulate. In order to paint his portrait, Luke drew upon his literary abilities, which included the skills of rhetoric and its embedded values. The evidence, I argue, clearly shows that Luke attempted to portray Jesus' death as noble, according to the values of Greco-Roman society.

8. *Suggested Future Directions*

Luke apparently found parts of the passion narratives of Matthew and Mark inadequate for his purpose. As an apologist for the faith, he perceived a need to redeem Jesus' reputation and to emphasize his virtuous courage in the face of death. Jesus' courage and control during his passion is often said to be related to Luke's 'high Christology', the type we see most prominently in the Fourth Gospel. Yet

123. Soards, 'The Historical and Cultural Setting of Luke–Acts', 47.

Luke's more pressing motivation was to present Jesus as palatable to an audience steeped in Greco-Roman values. It would be interesting to see whether the Lukan passion did in fact have an influence in the way that subsequent Christian apologists defended the Christian faith. If not, why? Origen, for one, had to defend Christianity against Celsus' charges that its founder was timid, weak, and less than noble. One wonders whether Origen knew the Gospel of Luke, and if he did, why did he not make more use of it in his defense of Christianity?

This study may also suggest further links between Luke and Greco-Roman biography. Of the four canonical Gospels, Luke's relationship to Hellenistic literature is most readily acknowledged. Since Luke is evidently concerned with Jesus' praiseworthy status, we might ask to what extent the Gospel as a whole is indebted to encomiastic biography.

9. *Personal Reflections*

One of the questions which this study raises for me is whether Luke's use of noble death motifs makes his passion less authentic. Are we, in Luke, a step removed from the true story? Does the Lukan passion suffer because Jesus does not? Do we lose some of Jesus' humanity and his human weakness when we picture him as the courageous man of the noble death? Compared to Matthew and Mark, is the Lukan Jesus less compelling? Does his unemotional approach to the cross somehow separate him from the modern man? Perhaps such questions miss the larger point. Luke most probably understood his Gospel less as a rebuttal of the Matthean//Markan account than as a supplemental corrective. The Matthean//Markan Jesus is powerful because he knows what it is to suffer. The Lukan Jesus is compelling because he knows what it is to persevere and remain unbowed. Luke would offer Jesus as a model, so that the reader might take heart in his courage. The one who is put to death on a shameful cross is the glorious one who confers his benefits and remains victorious. He is worthy of honor and praise.

BIBLIOGRAPHY

Adkins, A.W.H., *Merit and Responsibility: A Study in Greek Values* (Oxford: Oxford University Press, 1960).

—*Moral Values and Political Behaviour in Ancient Greece: From Homer to the End of the Fifth Century* (New York: W.W. Norton, 1972).

Ahrensdorf, Peter J., *The Death of Socrates and the Life of Philosophy: An Interpretation of Plato's Phaedo* (Albany: State University of New York Press, 1995).

Alexander, L.C.A., 'Luke's Preface in the Context of Greek Preface-Writing', *NovT* 28.1 (1986), 48-74.

—'The Preface of Acts and the Historians', in Ben Witherington, III (ed.), *History, Literature, and Society in the Book of Acts* (Cambridge: Cambridge University Press, 1996), 73-103.

The Ante-Nicene Fathers (Grand Rapids: Eerdmans, 1885).

Aschermann, Hartmut, 'Zum Agoniegebet Jesu, Luk. 22,43-44', *ThViat* 5 (1953–54), 143-49.

Aune, David, *The New Testament in its Literary Environment* (Philadelphia: Westminster Press, 1987).

Baldwin, C.S., *Medieval Rhetoric and Poetic* (New York: Macmillan, 1928).

Barker, Andrew, 'Why did Socrates Refuse to Escape?', *Phronesis* 22 (1977), 13-28.

Barrow, R.H., *Plutarch and his Times* (Bloomington: Indiana University Press, 1967).

Bauernsseind, Otto, 'ἀρετή', in *TDNT*, I, 458-61.

Beck, B.E., '"Imitatio Christi" and the Lucan Passion Narrative', in W. Horbury and B. McNeil (eds.), *Suffering and Martyrdom in the New Testament: Studies for G.M. Styler* (Cambridge: Cambridge University Press, 1981), 28-47.

Benz, E., 'Christ und Sokrates in der alten Kirche: Ein Beitrag zum altkirchlichen Verständnis des Märtyrers und des Märtyriums', *ZNW* (1950–51), 195-224.

Berger, Klaus, 'Hellenistische Gattungen und Neues Testaments', in *ANRW*, II 23,2, 1031-32, 1831-85.

Bock, Darrell L., *Blasphemy and Exaltation in Judaism: The Charge against Jesus in Mark 14.53-65* (Grand Rapids: Baker Book House, 2000).

—*Proclamation from Prophecy and Pattern: Lucan Old Testament Christology* (JSNTSup, 12; Sheffield: JSOT Press, 1987).

Bonner, Stanley F., *Education in Ancient Rome: From the Elder Cato to the Younger Pliny* (Berkeley: University of California Press, 1977).

Braun, Will, *Feasting and Social Rhetoric in Luke 14* (Cambridge: Cambridge University Press, 1995.

Brown, Raymond, *The Birth of the Messiah: A Commentary on the Gospels of Matthew and Luke* (ABRL; Garden City, NY: Doubleday, rev. edn, 1993).

– *The Death of the Messiah: From Gethsemane to the Grave* (2 vols.; Garden City, NY: Doubleday, 1994).

Brown, Schuyler, *Apostasy and Perseverance in the Theology of Luke* (AnBib, 36; Rome: Pontifical Biblical Institute, 1969).
Bultmann, Rudolf, *History of the Synoptic Tradition* (trans. John Marsh; New York: Harper & Row, 1976).
Burgess, Theodore, *Epideictic Literature* (ed. Leonardo Taran; New York: Garland, 1987).
—'Epideictic Rhetoric', *Studies in Classical Philology* 3 (1902), 89-261; reprinted as *Epideictic Literature* (New York: Garland Publishing, 1987).
Burridge, Richard A., *What are the Gospels? A Comparison with Graeco-Roman Biography* (Cambridge: Cambridge University Press, 1992).
Butts, James, 'The Progymnasmata of Theon: A New Text with Translation and Commentary' (unpublished dissertation; Claremont University, CA, 1987).
Cadbury, Henry J., *The Making of Luke–Acts* (Peabody, MA: Hendrickson, 1958).
Cassidy, Richard, and Phillip Scharper (eds.), *Political Issues in Luke–Acts* (Maryknoll, NY: Orbis Books, 1983).
Collins, Adela Yarbo, 'From Noble Death to Crucified Messiah', *NTS* 40 (1994), 481-503.
—'The Genre of the Passion Narrative', *Studia Theologica: Scandanavia Journal of Theology* 47 (1993), 3-28.
Conzelmann, Hans, *Acts of the Apostles: A Commentary on the Acts of the Apostles* (trans. James Limburgh, A. Thomas Kraabel, and Donald H. Juel; Philadelphia: Fortress Press, 1987).
—*The Theology of St. Luke* (London: Macmillan, 1960).
Cox, Patricia, *Biography in Late Antiquity: A Quest for the Holy Man* (Berkeley: University of California Press, 1983).
—*Development of Greek Biography* (Berkeley: University of California Press, 1983).
Cullman, Oscar, 'Immortality of the Soul or Resurrection of the Dead: The Witness of the New Testament', in Krister Stendahl (ed.), *Immortality and Resurrection* (New York: Macmillan, 1965), 12-20.
Danker, Frederick, *Benefactor: Epigraphic Study of a Graeco-Roman and New Testament Semantic Field* (St Louis: Clayton Publishing House, 1982).
—*Jesus and the New Age: A Commentary on St. Luke's Gospel* (Philadelphia: Fortress Press, 1988).
Delatte, A., 'Le sage-témoin dans la philosophie stoïco-cynique', *Bulletin de la classe des lettres et de sciences morales et politiques de l'Acadmie Royale de Belgique* 39 (1953), 166-86.
Delobel, J., 'L'onction par la pecheresse', *ETL* 42 (1969), 415-75.
deSilva, David A., *Despising Shame: Honor Discourse and Community Maintenance in the Epistle to the Hebrews* (SBLDS, 152; Atlanta: Scholars Press, 1995).
Dibelius, Martin, *From Tradition to Gospel* (London: Macmillan, 1934).
Dodds, E.R., *Greeks and the Irrational* (Berkeley: University of California Press, 1951).
—*Pagan and Christian in an Age of Anxiety* (Cambridge: Cambridge University Press, 1951).
Doran, Robert, *Temple Propaganda: The Purpose and Character of 2 Maccabees* (CBQMS, 12; Washington, DC: Catholic Biblical Association of America, 1981).

Döring, Klaus, *Exemplum Socratis: Studien zur Sokratesnachwirkung in der kynisch-stoischen Popularphilosophie der frühen Kaiserzeit und im frühen Christentum* (Hermes, Zeitschrift für klassische Philologie, Einzelschriften, 42; Wiesbaden: Steiner, 1979).

Dover, K.J., *Greek Popular Morality in the Time of Plato and Aristotle* (Berkeley: University of California Press, 1974).

Downing, F.G., 'Jesus and Martyrdom', *JTS* 14 (1963), 546-59.

Droge, Arthur J., 'Mori Lucrum: Paul and Ancient Theories of Suicide', *NovT* 30 (1988), 263-86.

Droge, Arthur J., and James D. Tabor, *A Noble Death: Suicide and Martyrdom among Christians and Jews in Antiquity* (San Francisco: HarperSanFrancisco, 1992).

Ehrman, Bart, and Mark Plunkett, 'The Angel and the Agony: The Textual Problem of Luke 22.43-44', *CBQ* 45 (1983), 401-16.

Ernst, J., *Das Evangelium nach Lukas* (Regensburg: Pustet, 1974).

Fascher, J.M., 'Sokrates und Christus', *ZNW* 45 (1954), 1-41.

Feuillet, A., *L'Agonie de Gethsémani: Enquête exégétique et théologique suivie d'une étude du 'Mystère de Jésus' de Pascal* (Paris: J. Gabalda, 1977).

Fitzgerald, John T., *Cracks in an Earthen Vessel: An Examination of the Catalogues of Hardships in the Corinthian Correspondence* (SBLDS, 99; Atlanta: Scholars Press, 1988).

Fitzmyer, Joseph A., 'Crucifixion in Ancient Palestine, Qumran Literature, and the New Testament', *CBQ* 40 (1978), 493-513.

—*Luke the Theologian: Aspects of his Teaching* (New York: Paulist Press, 1989).

—*The Gospel according to Luke* (AB, 28, 28A; 2 vols.; Garden City, NY: Doubleday, 1985).

Ford, J. Massyngbaerde, *My Enemy is my Guest: Jesus and Violence in Luke* (Maryknoll, NY: Orbis Books, 1984).

Frend, William Hugh Clifford, *Martyrdom and Persecution in the Early Church: A Study of a Conflict from the Maccabees to Donatus* (Oxford: Basil Blackwell, 1965).

Garrison, Elise P., 'Attitudes toward Suicide in Ancient Greece', *Transactions of the American Philological Association* 121 (1991), 1-34.

Giankaris, C.J., *Plutarch* (New York: Twayne Publishers, 1970).

Goldstein, J.A., *II Maccabees* (AB, 41A; Garden City, NY: Doubleday, 1983).

Grundmann, Walter, 'δεῖ, δέον, ἐστί', in *TDNT*, II, 21-25.

Güttgemans, Erhardt, 'In welchem Sinne ist Lukas "Historiker"? Die Beziehungen von Luk 1, 1-4 und Papias zur antiken Rhetorik', *LingBib* 54 (1983), 9-26.

Gwynn, Aubrey, *Roman Education from Cicero to Quintilian* (Oxford: Clarendon Press, 1926).

Hadas, Moses, *Aristeas to Philocrates* (New York: Ktav, 1973).

—*The Third and Fourth Books of Maccabees* (New York: Ktav, 1976).

Harrington, W.J., *The Gospel according to St. Luke* (London: Geoffrey Chapman, 1968).

Hauck, Friedrich, 'ὑπομένη', in *TDNT*, IV, 581-88.

Hemer, Colin J., *The Book of Acts in the Setting of Hellenistic History* (Tübingen: J.C.B. Mohr, 1989).

Hengel, Martin, *Crucifixion: In the Ancient World and the Folly of the Message of the Cross* (Philadelphia: Fortress Press, 1977).
Henten, Jan Willem, van, *The Maccabean Martyrs as Saviours of the Jewish People: A Study of 2 and 4 Maccabees* (Leiden: E.J. Brill, 1997).
Hock, Ronald F., and Edward N. O'Neil, *The Chreia in Ancient Rhetoric.* I. *The Progymnasmata* (SBLTT, 27; Greco-Roman Religion, 9; Atlanta: Scholars Press, 1986).
Holleran, J. Warren, *The Synoptic Gethsemane: A Critical Study* (Rome: Università Gregoriana Editrice, 1973).
Hoof, A.J.L. van, *From Autothanasia to Suicide: Self Killing in Classical Antiquity* (London: Routledge, 1990).
Horst, P.W. van der, 'Hellenistic Parallels to the Acts of the Apostles', *JSNT* 25 (1985), 59-60.
Jaeger, Werner, *Paideia: The Ideals of Greek Culture* (3 vols.; New York: Oxford University Press, 1943).
Johnson, Luke T., *Acts of the Apostles* (Collegeville, MN: Liturgical Press, 1992).
Jones, C.P., *Plutarch and Rome* (Oxford: Clarendon Press, 1971).
Just, Arthur A., Jr, *Luke* (Concordia Commentary; Saint Louis: Concordia Publishing House, 1996).
Karris, Robert J., *Luke: Artist and Theologian: Luke's Passion Account as Literature* (New York: Paulist Press, 1985).
Kennedy, George, *The Art of Persuasion in Greece* (Princeton, NJ: Princeton University Press, 1963).
—*The Art of Persuasion in the Roman World: 300 B.C.–A.D. 300* (Princeton, NJ: Princeton University Press, 1963).
—*The Art of Rhetoric in the Roman World: 300 B.C. – A.D. 300* (Princeton, NJ: Princeton University Press, 1972).
—*A New History of Classical Rhetoric* (Princeton, NJ: Princeton University Press, 1994).
—*New Testament Interpretation through Rhetorical Criticism* (Chapel Hill, NC: University of North Carolina Press, 1984).
Kilpatrick, G.D., 'A Theme of the Lucan Passion Story and Luke xxiii. 47', *JTS* 43 (1942), 34-36.
Kloppenborg, John, 'Exitus clari viri: The Death of Jesus in Luke', *TJT* 8 (1992), 106-20.
Kurz, W.S., 'Luke 22.14-38 and Greco-Roman and Biblical Farewell Addresses', *JBL* 104 (1985), 251-68.
Lagrange, M.J., *Evangile selon Saint Luc* (Paris: J. Gabalda, 1927).
Lentz, T.M., *Orality and Literacy in Hellenic Culture* (Carbondale: Southern Illinois University Press, 1989).
Liddell, Henry George, and Robert Scott, *Greek–English Lexicon* (Oxford: Clarendon Press, 1986).
Lohse, E., *Märtyrien in jüdischer und frühchristlicher Zeit* (Göttingen: Vandenhoeck & Ruprecht, 1938.
Loisy, A., *L'évangile selon Luc* (Paris: E. Nourry, 1924; repr., Frankfurt: Minerva, 1971).
Loraux, Nicole, *The Invention of Athens: The Funeral Oration in the Classical City* (Cambridge, MA: Harvard University Press, 1986).

Mack, Burton L., *Rhetoric and the New Testament* (Minneapolis: Fortress Press, 1990).

Mack, Burton L., and Vernon K. Robbins, 'Elaboration of the Chreia in the Hellenistic School', in *iidem* (eds.), *Patterns of Persuasion in the Gospel* (Sonoma, CA: Polebridge Press, 1989), 31-67.

Malherbe, Abraham J., '"Not in a Corner": Early Christian Apologetic in Acts 26.26', *The Second Century* 5 (1985–86), 193-210.

Malina, Bruce, *The New Testament World: Insights from Cultural Anthropology* (Louisville, KY: Westminster/John Knox Press, rev. edn, 1993).

—'Patron and Client: The Analogy Behind Synoptic Theology', *Foundations and Facets Forum* 4.1 (1988), 2-32.

Malina, Bruce, and Jerome Neyrey, 'Honor and Shame in Luke–Acts', in Neyrey (ed.), *The Social World of Luke–Acts*, 25-66.

—*Portraits of Paul: An Archaeology of Ancient Personality* (Louisville, KY: Westminster/John Knox Press, 1993).

Marrou, H.I., *A History of Education in Antiquity* (New York: Sheed & Ward, 1956).

Martin, Josef, *Symposion: Die Geschichte einer literarischen Form* (Paderborn: Schöningh, 1931).

Mason, Steve, *Josephus and the New Testament* (Peabody, MA: Hendrickson, 1992).

Matera, F.J., 'The Death of Jesus according to Luke: A Question of Sources', *CBQ* (1985), 469-85.

—*Passion Narratives and Gospel Theologies* (New York: Paulist Press, 1986).

Matill, Jr, A.J., 'The Jesus-Paul Parallels and the Purpose of Luke–Acts', *NovT* 17 (1975), 15-46.

Matsen, Patricia P., Philip Rollinson, and Marion Sousa, *Readings from Classical Rhetoric* (Carbondale: Southern Illinois University Press, 1990).

Menander Rhetor (eds. D.A. Russell and Nigel Wilson; Oxford: Clarendon Press, 1981).

Momigliano, Arnoldo, *Development of Greek Biography* (Cambridge, MA: Harvard University Press, 1971).

Moxnes, Halvor, 'Honour and Righteousness in Romans', *JSNT* 32 (1988), 61-77.

Musurillo, H.A., *The Acts of the Pagan Martyrs: Acta Alexandrinorum* (Oxford: Oxford University Press, 1954; repr. edn, New York: Arno, 1979).

Nadeau, Ray, 'The Progymnasmata of Aphthonius in Translation', *Speech Monographs* 19 (1952), 264-85.

Navia, Luis E., *Socratic Testimonies* (Latham, MD: University Press of America, 1987).

Neyrey, Jerome, 'The Absence of Jesus' Emotions—Lukan Redaction of Lk. 22, 39-46', *Bib* 61 (1980), 153-71.

—'Acts 17, Epicureans and Theodicy: A Study in Stereotypes', in D. Balch and W. Meeks (eds.), *Greeks, Romans, and Christians: Essays in Honor of Abraham J. Malherbe* (Minneapolis: Fortress Press, 1990), 127-39.

—'"Despising the Shame of the Cross": Honor and Shame in the Johannine Passion Narrative', *Semeia* 68 (1996), 113-37.

—'The Forensic Defense Speech in Acts 22–26: Form and Function', in Charles H. Talbert (ed.), *Luke–Acts: New Perspectives from the Society of Biblical Literature Seminar* (New York: Crossroad, 1984), 210-24.

—*Honor and Shame in the Gospel of Matthew* (Louisville, KY: Westminster/John Knox Press, 1998).
—'Josephus' Vita and the Encomium: A Native Model of Personality', *JSJ* 25.2 (1990), 177-206.
Neyrey, Jerome (ed.), *The Passion according to Luke: A Redaction Study of Luke's Soteriology* (New York: Paulist Press, 1985).
—*The Social World of Luke–Acts: Models for Interpretation* (Peabody, MA: Hendrickson, 1991).
Nolland, John, *Luke* (3 vols.; Dallas: Word Books, 1993).
O'Toole, Robert, 'Luke's Position on Politics and Society in Luke–Acts', in Cassidy and Scharper (eds.), *Political Issues in Luke–Acts*, 1-17.
—*The Unity of Luke's Theology* (Wilmington, DE: Michael Glazier, 1984).
Pangle, Thomas L., 'Socrates in Xenophon's Political Writings', in Waerdt (ed.), *The Socratic Movement*, 127-50.
Parsons, Mikeal C., 'Luke and the *Progymnasmata*: A Preliminary Investigation into the Preliminary Exercises', in Todd Penner and Caroline Vander Stichele (eds.), *Contextualizing Acts: Lukan Narrative and Greco-Roman Discourse* (SBLSP, 20; Atlanta: Society of Biblical Literature, 2003), 43-65.
Pearson, Lionel, *Popular Ethics in Ancient Greece* (Stanford: Stanford University Press, 1962).
Pilch, John J., 'Sickness and Healing in Luke–Acts', in Neyrey (ed.), *The Social World of Luke–Acts*, 181-209.
Plymale, Steven F., *Prayer Texts of Luke* (New York: Peter Lang, 1991).
Polhill, John B., *Acts: The New American Commentary* (Nashville: Broadman Press, 1992).
Potter, D., 'Martyrdom as Spectacle', in R. Scodel (ed.), *Theater and Society in the Classical World* (Ann Arbor: University of Michigan Press, 1993), 53-88.
Renehan, R., 'The Greek Philosophic Background of Fourth Maccabees', *Rheinisches Museum für Philologie* 115 (1972), 223-38.
Rengstorf, Karl H., *Das Evangelium nach Lukas* (Göttingen: Vandenhoeck & Ruprecht, 1962).
Reumann, J.H., 'Psalm 22 at the Cross', *Interpretation* 28 (1974), 39-58.
Richard, Earl (ed.), *New Views on Luke and Acts* (Collegeville, MN: Liturgical Press [A Michael Glazier Book], 1990).
Ringe, Sharon, *Luke* (Louisville, KY: Westminster/John Knox Press, 1995).
Robbins, Vernon K., 'Prefaces in Greco-Roman Biography and Luke–Acts', in Paul Achtemeier (ed.), *Society of Biblical Literature 1978 Seminar Papers* (Missoula, MT: Scholars Press, 1978), 193-207.
—'The Social Location of the Implied Author of Luke–Acts', in Neyrey (ed.), *The Social World of Luke–Acts*, 305-22.
—'Writing as a Rhetorical Act in Plutarch and the Gospels', in Duanne Watson (ed.), *Persuasive Artistry: Studies in New Testament Rhetoric in Honor of George A. Kennedy* (JSNTSup, 50; Sheffield: JSOT Press, 1991), 157-86.
Rohrbaugh, Richard, 'The Pre-industrial City in Luke–Acts', in Neyrey (ed.), *The Social World of Luke–Acts*, 125-49.
Ronconi, Alessandro, 'Exitus illustrium virorum', *RAC* 6 (1966), 1258-66.
Rowe, Christopher, *An Introduction to Greek Ethics* (London: Harper & Row, 1976).

Russel, D.A., *On Reading Plutarch's Lives* (Berkeley: University of California Press, 1974).
—*Plutarch* (London: Gerald Duckworth, 1973).
—'Progymnasmata', in *The Oxford Classical Dictionary* (Oxford: Clarendon Press, 2nd edn, 1962), 883.
Sandnes, Karl Olav, 'Paul and Socrates: The Aim of Paul's Areopagus Speech', *JSNT* 59 (1993), 13-26.
Schlier, Heinrich, 'παρρησία', in *TDNT*, V, 871-86.
Schmidt, D., 'Luke's "Innocent" Jesus: A Scriptural Apologetic', in Cassidy and Scharper (eds.), *Political Issues in Luke Acts*, 111-21.
Schmidt, Karl L., 'Die Stellung der Evangelien in der allgemeinene Literaturgeschichte', in Hans Schmidt (ed.), *Eucharisterion: Studien zur Religion und Literatur des Alten und Neuen Testaments: Herman Gunkel zum 60 Geburtstag* (Göttingen: Vandenhoeck & Ruprecht, 1923), 50-134.
Schrenk, Gottlob, 'διαλέγομαι', in *TDNT*, II, 93-95.
Scott, James, 'Luke's Geographical Horizon', in David W.J. Gill and Conrad Gempf (eds.), *The Book of Acts in its Graeco-Roman Setting* (*The Book of Acts in its First Century Setting*, 2; Grand Rapids: Eerdmans, 1994), 483-544.
Seeley, David, *The Noble Death: Graeco-Roman Martyrology and Paul's Concept of Salvation* (JSNTSup, 28; Sheffield: JSOT Press, 1989).
Senior, Donald, *The Passion of Jesus in the Gospel of Luke* (Wilmington, DE: Michael Glazier, 1989).
Shea, G.W., 'On the Burial of Jesus in Mark 15.42-47', *Faith & Reason* 17 (1991), 87-108.
Shuler, Philip L., *A Genre for the Gospels: The Biographical Character of Matthew* (Philadelphia: Fortress Press, 1982).
—'Genre(s) for the Gospels', in D.L. Dugan (ed.), *The Interrelations of the Gospels* (Leuven: University Press, 1990), 459-83.
Soards, Marion, 'The Historical and Cultural Setting of Luke–Acts', in Richard (ed.), *New Views on Luke and Acts*, 33-47.
—'A Literary Analysis of the Origin and Purpose of Luke's Account of the Mockery of Jesus', in Richard (ed.), *New Views on Luke and Acts*, 86-93.
—*The Passion according to Luke: The Special Material of Luke 22* (JSNTSup, 14; Sheffield: JSOT Press, 1995).
—*The Speeches in Acts: Their Content, Context, and Concerns* (Louisville, KY: Westminster/John Knox Press, 1994).
Sourvinou-Inwood, Christiane, *'Reading' Greek Death: To the End of the Classical Period* (Oxford: Oxford University Press, 1995).
Spengel, Leonard, *Rhetores Graeci*, II (Leipzig: Teubner, 1854).
Springs Steele, E., 'Luke 11.37-54—A Modified Hellenistic Symposium?', *JBL* 103 (1984), 379-94.
Stauffer, Karl L., 'ἀγών', in *TDNT*, I, 134-40.
Stein, Robert, *Luke* (Nashville: Broadman Press, 1992).
Stein, Siegfried, 'The Influence of Symposia Literature on the Literary Form of the Pesah Haggada', *JJS* 8 (1957), 13-44.
Sterling, Gregory, *Historiography and Self-Definition: Josephos, Luke–Acts and Apologetic Historiography* (SNT, 64; Leiden: E.J. Brill, 1992).
—'Mors philosophi: The Death of Jesus in Luke', *HTR* 94 (2001): 383-402.

Stewart, Zeph, 'Greek Crowns and Christian Martyrs', in Patrick Cramer (ed.), *Mémorial André-Jean Festugière* (Geneva: Genève Press, 1984), 119-24.

Stöger, Alois, 'Eigenart und Botschaft der lukanischen Passiongeschichte', *BK* 24 (1965), 5-6.

Streeter, B.H., *The Four Gospels: A Study of Origins* (London: Macmillan, 1927).

Surkau, H.W., *Martyrien in jüdischer und frühchristlicher Zeit* (Göttingen: Vandenhoeck & Ruprecht, 1938).

Sylva, Dennis D., 'The Temple Curtain and Jesus' Death in the Gospel of Luke', *JBL* 105 (1986), 239-50.

Talbert, Charles H., *Literary Patterns, Theological Themes and the Genre of Luke–Acts* (SBLMS, 20; Missoula, MT: Scholars Press, 1974).

—'Martyrdom in Luke–Acts and the Lukan Social Ethic', in Cassidy and Scharper (eds.), *Political Issues in Luke–Acts*, 99-110.

—*Reading Luke: A Literary and Theological Commentary on the Third Gospel* (New York: Crossroad, 1982).

—*Reading Acts: A Literary and Theological Commentary on the Acts of the Apostles* (New York: Crossroad, 1997).

—*What is a Gospel? The Genre the Canonical Gospels* (Philadelphia: Fortress Press, 1977).

Tannehill, Robert C., *Luke* (Nashville: Abingdon Press, 1996).

—*The Narrative Unity of Luke–Acts: A Literary Interpretation* (Philadelphia: Fortress Press, 1986).

Taylor, Vincent, *The Passion Narrative of St. Luke: A Critical and Historical Investigation* (Cambridge: Cambridge University Press, 1972).

Thackeray, H.St. John, *Josephus: The Man and the Historian* (New York: Ktav, 1967).

Tyson, Joseph B., *The Death of Jesus in Luke–Acts* (Columbia: University of South Carolina Press, 1986).

Waerdt, Paul A. Vander, *The Socratic Movement* (Ithaca, NY: Cornell University Press, 1994).

Walaskay, P.W., *'And So We Came to Rome': The Political Perspective of St. Luke* (SNTSMS, 49; Cambridge: Cambridge University Press, 1972).

Wardman, Alan, *Plutarch's Lives* (Berkeley: University of California Press, 1974).

Watson, Duane, 'Writing as a Rhetorical Act in Plutarch and the Gospels', in *idem* (ed.), *Persuasive Artistry: Studies in New Testament Rhetoric in Honor of George A. Kennedy* (JSNTSup, 50; Sheffield: JSOT Press, 1991).

Weinrich, William, *Spirit and Martyrdom: A Study of the Work of the Holy Spirit in Contexts of Persecution and Martyrdom in the New Testament and Early Christian Literature* (Washington, DC: University Press of America, 1981).

Westerink, Leendert G., *The Greek Commentaries on Plato's Phaedo* (Amsterdam: North-Holland).

Wilckens, Ulrich, 'σοφία', in *TDNT*, VII, 465-96.

Williams, Sam K., *Jesus' Death as Saving Event: The Background and Origin of a Concept* (Missoula, MT: Scholars Press, 1975).

Winter, S.C., 'ΠΑΡΡΗΣΙΑ in Acts', in John T. Fitzgerald (ed.), *Friendship, Flattery, and Frankness of Speech: Studies in the New Testament World* (Leiden: E.J. Brill, 1996), 185-202.

Woozley, Anthony D., *Law and Obedience: The Arguments of Plato's Crito* (Chapel Hill: University of North Carolina Press, 1979).

—'Socrates on Disobeying the Law', in G. Vlastos (ed.), *The Philosophy of Socrates* (New York: Macmillan, 1972).
Yaghjian, Lucretia, 'Ancient Reading', in Richard Rohrbaugh (ed.), *The Social Sciences and New Testament Interpretation* (Peabody, MA: Hendrickson, 1996), 206-30.
Zeitlin, Solomon, *The Second Book of Maccabees: With Introduction and Summary* (New York: Harper & Bros., 1954).
Ziolkowski, John, *Thucydides and the Tradition of Funeral Speeches at Athens* (New York: Arno Press, 1981).
Zweck, D., 'The Exordium of the Areopagus Speech, Acts 17.22-23', *NTS* 35 (1989), 94-103.

Indexes

Index of References

INDEX OF AUTHORS

Printed in the United States
78145LV00002BB/253

9 781905 048243